A Script for Aspiring Women Leaders

Download Free Workbook
with additional forms and worksheets
at www.markvillareal.com/aspiringwomen.

A Script for

Aspiring Women
Leaders

5 Keys To Success

Mark Villareal
and Crystal Ann Suniga

ISBN: 978-1-7323085-7-2

Copyright © 2020 by Mark Villareal

CONTENTS

FOREWORD
NANCY MATTHEWS

It comes as no surprise to anyone that there is a disparity between the number of men and women in leadership positions and that great efforts must be undertaken by both men and women to create balance and equal representation in both business and government.

The effort to be taken by women is the process of embracing our gifts and skills as leaders and expanding our roles to the boardrooms and beyond.

The effort to be taken by men is a process of allowing and agreement that increasing the number of women in leadership positions creates benefits for the good of all.

One of the challenges I faced in growing into the leader I am today, and a major impetus to the creation of my company, Women's Prosperity Network, was the absence of female role models. My mother, a stellar executive assistant, was my role model for my career path. She instilled a strong work ethic and desire to grow and often reminded me of the importance of learning shorthand and being able to type. "As long as you can type, you'll always be able to get a job." While the message was important (and true ... I am a fast typist!), it also carried a subliminal message of what I "could" be.

What if the reminders and lessons from my mother were focused on the steps that Mark & Crystal guide us through in this book? How much faster would my rise in leadership and 'coming into my own' have been? How many more women would I have been able to be a role model and mentor for had I embarked on my leadership journey earlier?

I honor my mother and all that she instilled in me. Let's face it, she didn't have women leaders as role models either! Fortunately, in my late 30's I was introduced to mentors and coaches that encouraged me to dream big and who also gave me step-by-step instructions.

The knowledge you hold in your hands is a roadmap to your rise in leadership. You already have the gifts, you already have the desire, the next step is up to you. With this roadmap you get to chart your own course and pave the way for other women. Thank you for answering the call to rise in leadership. We need you!

"The world will be saved by the western woman."

—Dalai Lama

Nancy Matthews
Co-Founder, Women's Prosperity Network
International Speaker, Best-Selling Author
Business Consultant & Master Coach

FOREWORD
ELLEN VOIE

Don't let the title fool you, as this book is not only for women, and it's not just for leaders! If you don't find valuable information to help you organize the rest of your life, then you're not paying attention.

Mark Villareal and Crystal Ann Suniga walk you through a process that will be life-changing. The story is related through the lens of a mentorship program. The narrator begins by introducing us to Ann, an "aspiring female leader" working in an administrative position.

Ann is guided through a process that is sometimes painful, but more often, insightful. She is asked to write a personal mission statement, something every one of us should be doing already. Just as our businesses have mission statements that guide our actions, so should we, as individuals.

The process continues with an exercise to create principle statements, which differ from a mission as defined by the authors, as turning your values into action proclamations. Each step in the narration includes Ann's thought progression as she struggles to determine what is important to her.

For Ann, which is typical for many women, a greater focus on her career caused challenges at home as her husband and son expressed their feelings of being abandoned as she spends more time and effort on her leadership goals. The book even offers advice on addressing this marital discord through difficult conversations from Ann's mentors who have experienced these challenges.

Throughout the book, you will find worksheets, spreadsheets, and evaluation forms for the reader to complete alongside Ann as she struggles through these thought-provoking deliberations. She honestly reviews her leadership traits and establishes a plan to address areas needing improvement.

You could spend thousands of dollars on hiring a leadership coach, or you can pick up *A Script for Aspiring Women Leaders: 5 Keys to Success.* This book provides a detailed road map for you to follow as you start your journey to achieve greater success in both your personal and professional life. Regardless of where you are in your career, you will find a renewed focus in defining yourself and your goals.

Ellen Voie, CAE, PDC
Founder, Women In Trucking Association, Inc.
www.womenintrucking.org/

Women In Trucking Association's mission is to encourage the employment of women in the trucking industry, promote their accomplishments, and minimize obstacles faced by women working in the trucking industry.

FOREWORD
MARSH ENGLE

I found myself standing in front of a stage linking arms with ONE MILLION change-makers. Behind the mic, the dynamic Grammy Award winning recording artist, Alicia Keys. Her words to us, a call to leadership ...

Fire in our belly. Feet on the ground.

That was 2017. The first year of the WOMEN'S MARCH in Washington DC. She was inspiring each of us to action ... individually expressed, collectively creators of change.

What I've come to know to be true is that *'feet on the ground'* looks different for everyone and carries many unique expressions. What's important is that we answer our call to lead, authentically and unapologetically.

It's a time for noticing the world around you.
Studying the shifts required.
It's a time for putting your genius into action and making choices that
speak to providing new ideas and answers.

Driving Innovation. Implementing influential ideas. Trailblazing change.

Collaboration driven. Value focused. Creativity fueled.

These are the trademarks of the new wave of a woman leader.

We need not look too far to recognize there's a substantial shift underway and it's the woman who develops a strong and dynamic platform of success leadership who will lead the way. She knows who she is and where she is going. And, at the core of this clarity is the empowered capacities to elevate the workplace, motivate transformation, and generate impact.

When it comes to your career or growing your business,
authenticity is key. Be direct and very clear about
what success looks like for you.

By mastering the foundations provided within the pages of this book, you'll find a roadmap to define a strong identity and determine how you will create your personal and professional future—elevating the definition of your role and your expertise—encapsulating your strengths—all essential to enhancing your individual authentic style of success leadership.

"There comes a time when a woman can no longer deny her call to
lead. A time when her voice vibrant. The truth of her value realized.
She knows the undeniable power of putting her creativity into action.
She knows that she is standing at the threshold of living purpose-
powered, mission-driven success.
That time is now!"

As we link arms together and rise in our creative contributions, I'm fully committed be right there next to you—knowing that your time has come, our time has come. Together, as a nation of amazing women, we will lift one another into an inspired new future.

TOGETHER WE LEAD!

Marsh Engle
Founder, Amazing Woman Nation
www.theamazingwomannation.com/

Marsh Engle is an acclaimed visionary pioneer and a leading authority in the field of women's success bridging both the internal and external aspects of female power and contribution. A multi-published author of the bestselling AMAZING WOMAN book series and award-winning entrepreneur, her work and multi-decade research promotes practices to set free higher success—in career, in business, and in life. In 2016 Marsh served as an elected delegate to THE UNITED STATE OF WOMEN, an acclaimed leadership program sanctioned by THE WHITE HOUSE and led by First Lady Michelle Obama. She has shared the stage with bestselling authors including don Miguel Ruiz and Marianne Williamson; and the acclaimed journalist Maria Shriver. Marsh is the founder of AMAZING WOMAN NATION, an organization powered by MARSH ENGLE MEDIA, a diversified media company devoted to enhancing the lives of women by designing lifestyle content, training programs and products positioned to impact millions. For more information about Marsh Engle and her work, visit: www.AmazingWomanNation.com and www.MarshEngle.com.

INTRODUCTION
DR. CARMELA NANTON

Women's underrepresentation in leadership positions is no secret, and the research confirms that reality in many companies. Since women have historically faced barriers when they aspire to lead, the leadership culture, the type of leader and the aspirant's ambition must converge for her career advancement to prioritized. The leader's disposition, knowledge of their organization culture, and a personal operational philosophy of serving those who they lead are key factors. The leader must also be willing to use their power to support and sponsor the high-potential female candidate's growth and development. These are the characteristics of a Servant Leader. Servant leaders must also show foresight, which is an orientation to the future that they respond to by taking action to resolve organizational problems -while they can. There are three questions in the book *Servant Leadership*, that Greenleaf uses as a measure for recognizing servant leaders: Do those served grow as persons? Do they while being served become healthier, wiser, freer more autonomous, and more likely themselves to become servants? And what is the effect on the least privileged in society? Readers have opportunity to find the answers to each of these questions in the chapters of this book.

Leadership development of high-potential women candidates can take on several forms and one of these is mentoring. Given that about 95% of leaders at the executive level are male, *A Script for Aspiring Women Leaders: Five Keys to Success* illustrates a rare and excellent example of cross-gender mentoring in leadership development. The level of the executive leader in the organization is critical throughout the process because of the knowledge of the organization culture and the power of their sponsorship to communicate a message that influences organization-wide perception of the aspiring leader thus facilitating alignment between aspirant and organizational goals. This works best in formal mentor-protégé pairings but has value for informal mentoring relationships as well. The authors make the connection and application between women's natural leadership skills honed and refined through motherhood to contextualize concepts. Since leadership is not value neutral, 'inside out leading' or leading based on the leader's values and principles supports authenticity from the start. The leader-mentor serves as manager of the evolutionary process, guiding the aspirant 'protégé through development of their personal mission, vision, and goals and the intersection with organizational goals and the needed alignment for success. The process management role shifts to co-management with the protégé who ultimately becomes responsible for the process.

The book is useful in companies or can be adapted to coaching experiences for developing high-potential female talent. Methods that shape the 'protégé's leader identity development include the development of self-awareness with assessments that engage the input from those who work with the 'protégé, using targeted development questions, providing a rationale for responses and facilitating the thought-process through to ownership and action. Identifying and participating in support groups is vital in that they build her leadership capital, extending beyond the strong ties of family to expanded networks that accelerate and sustain ongoing development even in difficult times. Not all mentoring relationships are successful for a variety of reasons, as you might imagine. But the self-actualized outcomes can translate into internal and external opportunities. This book simultaneously integrates retrospective and futuristic approaches of the mentoring experience serving as a Coach's Blueprint for leadership development, complete with a step by step guide and process scripts for developing and empowering aspiring leaders.

Dr. Carmela Nanton
CEO of Carmel Connections, Inc.

Sources:
Greenleaf, R.K. *Servant Leadership: A journey into the nature of legitimate power and greatness.*

Dr. Carmela Nanton, CEO of Carmel Connections Inc., is a leadership strategist, executive coach, consultant, award-winning author, and educator. Diversity equity and inclusion, women's leadership. carmelconnections.com, carmelconnect@gmail.com, @DrCarmelaNanton, LI-FB/DrCarmelaNanton

A MESSAGE FROM
THE AUTHORS

"Behind every successful woman is a group of other successful women that have her back."

—Anonymous

Years of structure, culture, and embedded ways of status quo climbing the corporate ladder many may believe that it is still a man's world. We at times hear, "women are emotional, and men are logical." But is that belief reality? How can women with aspirations for leadership not only excel but even survive? The answer is simple, quit listening to the old beliefs and demonstrate your natural abilities and execute a plan that gets you noticed and recognized as a solid leader with solid traits for leadership. We have a very good friend who owns her own successful business whom we admire greatly for her leadership traits that we watch how she inspires others, is genuine, and has persevered in her own life. She stated that successful women do not believe they are competing with men. "The fact is, we are climbing our own ladder, sharing our own unique gifts and talents." This is what drives their success, and they support each other as mentioned in the above quote.

So what do women who aspire to be a leader do to advance? One, they set their mind straight as determination, perseverance and tenacity are all traits of a strong leader, and women possess these greatly. Next, they put a plan in place for them to develop in knowledge, skills, and awareness and execute to gain in each. They plan, like every great leader does, with goals, objectives, and create an outlook that they can believe in. They determine milestones so they can see a light at the end of the tunnel and see that progress is being made. Great leaders find mentors, and they mentor others as they learn from both sides of the equation. Like any organization, aspiring leaders need a mission, a reason for existence that gives them a purpose. They also need a vision that lays a challenge but also provides a guiding light. With everything comes a foundation of values and principles in which all decisions will be filtered through. In simple terms, they smartly build a solid foundation to build their success.

Crystal and I have seen that women have balanced skills that make strong leaders. The perception that women are emotional and men are logical is not accurate but only a view from the male perspective. Women have a more balanced level of traits that includes emotion and logic, along with higher levels of tenacity and perseverance. Also, they possess the additional traits of trust, integrity, ethics, honesty, loyalty, fun, and others that create strong skills in decision-making, coaching, and vision. Their hunger to learn and develop is matched by their desire to help support others. This book is our sharing of our mentoring model with the foundation building that contributes to success. We leave you with eye opening statistics from an article at Insead.edu from Suki Sohn.

What is the present state of women in leadership today?

- Women occupy 60% of junior positions
- Women occupy 50% of middle management
- Women occupy 20% of senior management
- Women occupy 10% of C-Suite executive roles
- Women occupy 5.1% of S&P 1500 CEO Roles
- Women account for only 10% of the short-term CEO candidate pool.

However, most gender diverse companies are 16% more likely to generate returns that are above the averages for their respective industries.

Chapter 1

DEFINE WHAT YOU WILL LIVE BY

Like the beginning of anything that you will build, you will always need to define what the foundation will be that you build upon. That foundation must be rooted in what defines you, as well as what you will live your life by. This foundation is instrumental in being a guide and a catalyst to every decision as well as every direction, strategy, initiative and roadblock that you will face. What you will live by must be ingrained in your heart so that it is automatic in your mind. This exercise is important. What you live by cannot be sacrificed as this is a promise that you make to yourself.

The first part of what you will live by comes from determining your personal values. This is where I teach that part of step one is defining your personal values and principles. My mother taught me over and over that values are what you live by and principles are what you stand on. What did she mean? What she meant was that some individuals find it effortless to name values as it sounds so easy. They throw around values like trust, integrity, ethics and honesty, which are all great values. But a principle is a value in action, and when a value becomes a principle it becomes automatic. I explain this in leadership as in business we get tested and sometimes an opportunity arises for short term gain, yet crosses the line of ethics. If ethics has grown to be a principle, the leader faced with that decision identifies the breach and eliminates it from consideration. We call this a moment of truth. A moment of truth for a leader arises many times, so this is why building your foundation is key.

Defining your values and principles:

This is an exercise where you truly need to do some soul searching. Assess your personal situation, what surrounds you, as well as what is important. Some values are easy to define and include as yours, but when defining them, I coach to list a sentence of why they are important to you. When mentoring an aspiring female leader named Ann who started in an administrative position, I would push her to dive deep on this issue. I would ask her the question 'why', over and over on the same topic. I explain this by utilizing an example of asking the question 'why' like a five-year-old. Working with Ann, whom I was mentoring, she defined her first value was respect. When I pushed on why respect was important to her, she first answered that respect was important because she wanted to demonstrate to others that she showed respect. That is legitimate, but the answer was external and I wanted to know why from an internal perspective. So I asked 'why'? She dug deeper and spoke of her son and her desire to teach him that respecting others was important, but also to be respected as something that is earned. She then opened up about her relationship and marriage where she struggled as she did not feel like she was always respected by her husband. Respect took a deeper meaning and we listed it out with her reasons why. Respect as a value resonated in her heart and hopefully in her mind that it would become a principle in action. She applied for the role of an administrative assistant as her confidence limited her on her belief of what she could accomplish. As I recognized her capabilities, I soon engaged in mentoring Ann to define if she had the hunger to develop past her confidence barrier. Women, who have been disrespected and dominated in relationships, are sometimes apprehensive to believe in what they can become. This is why respect was so important to Ann. As we worked on her next value she defined trust. As we pushed further into this value, we learned that teaching her son about trust was important. Once again, she had lost trust in her personal relationship from an instance of infidelity by her spouse as well as

Going deep on values sometimes brings out pain, but they truly define what is important.

additional reasons that he demonstrated. Going deep on values sometimes brings out pain, but they truly define what is important. The test will be if, when challenged, will the individual live by them? Ann and I worked more and she defined fun and passion as her next values. When pressed on why these two values, she believed that it was very important to her that she needed to have fun, and enjoy what she was doing. Besides, it was imperative that whatever she did, work or personal, that she have a passion for it. She wanted to demonstrate to her son this aspect, that in life you must pursue your passion. She admitted that she sacrificed this, and with mentoring, was gaining confidence to believe in herself again. The next value Ann defined was initiative. She and I defined with the process that she had limited her initiative and allowed others to place barriers around her. Once again, she determined that she wanted her son to seek and take initiative on his dreams and ideas and not let others hold him back. She realized that perhaps she had not been a good example in that area and now wanted to demonstrate through her initiative why it is important and how you can achieve. In addition, we defined that in any professional environment, which we were in, showing initiative was key to being successful and in growing to the next level. This was an important part of the values exercise, to push and determine different levels that values can have. Ann and I worked more and determined accountability was also an important value. Ann first defined it as self-accountability, as she wanted to hold herself accountable. As we pushed on her 'why', we also defined that being accountable to others, her son, her job, and yes, her spouse was important. We defined, as I coached, that accountability to others as a principle sometimes becomes hard when those others may not demonstrate accountability back. Accountability as a principle would commit Ann to be accountable even if others are not. You can see the importance of the exercise and the hard questions that have to be asked. As Ann and I worked further we defined her values as:

1. Respect
2. Trust
3. Fun
4. Passion
5. Initiative
6. Accountability
7. Hunger

The final value we determined was hunger, as Ann had admitted that she had lost her hunger and settled for less. The loss of hunger, or suppression of it, allowed her to be in others' control. It also allowed her to settle and not chase her dreams. Hunger is a great initiative. It is also common when mentoring aspiring women in leadership as hunger is key to empowerment. Now, certainly when executing the values exercise, one could name numerous values that make sense. I coach to keep the final list to seven or less, if possible. At times, we may list additional values during the exercise and push deeper on each to define 'the why.' This allowed us to then go back, review and narrow them to seven or less. This truly enhances the value of the exercise as the trimming down process drives focus and allows the individual to commit to the most important.

Once your values are defined, the next exercise is to create what we call Principle Statements. These are statements created by taking your values, in which you defined, and placing them in an action statement that completes the definition. These should be written with the individual in mind and always as a reminder for what they stand on. They can be as personal as possible or simplified. One technique I teach in my workbook on Mission, Vision and Values is to create a way to memorize each. We do this by creating a word taken from the first letter of each value, or with the letter that starts each Principle Statement. We call this creating a memorial word. So the first item to look at is if you can do this with the current values listed. With Ann's, we did not define that we could. So the next step was to define a word that was seven letters long that we could create Principle Statements from that would match. Reviewing seven letter words that matched Ann's belief system, we landed on respect. We laughed as we even thought of Aretha Franklin's song 'Respect'. So by defining this we see we can utilize some of the values whose first letter starts with one of the letters of respect. We then started to define the Principle Statements. In this exercise I coached Ann to make sure she is satisfied with each statement and to realize that each should define who she is. They should and need to be close and dear to the heart. So with the memorial word being respect, we started with the value of respect.

Principle Statements:

Value: Respect
Respect yourself first and demonstrate respect for others.

Value: Trust
Earn trust daily and reward others that do the same.

Value: Fun
Seek fun in all you do and let others enjoy and celebrate success.

Value: Passion
Passion is the objective, results are the achievement.

Value: Initiative
Execute with initiative and seek innovation.

Value: Accountability
Count accountability as your responsibility to yourself and others.

Value: Hunger
Taste the hunger for what feeds you and drives you to the next level.

You can see how Ann took these to the personal level that is close to her heart and automatic in her mind. The Principle Statements will help drive her as yours will drive you. You can clearly see that her principle statement of respect was truly personal to her and her situation. She wanted to challenge herself personally as well as professionally to understand her worth and to be treated with respect. With trust she realized it started with her first, but others have to earn it as well. She emphasized to have fun, as she must enjoy what she does. With passion, she defined her belief was her passion would drive results. She pushed herself with her statement to execute with initiative to always seek innovation. This includes her desire for accountability to be self-accountable first, she stated that in her statement. Finally, Ann wanted to remind herself daily to stay hungry, as well as what that meant to her. She defined that it is not just the hunger, but what feeds the hunger which is to develop and grow. With what was defined, we were able to create small wall signs for Ann to hang in her workplace as a constant reminder.

Respect yourself first and demonstrate respect for others.

Earn trust daily and reward others that do the same.

Seek fun in all you do and let others enjoy and celebrate success.

Passion is the objective, results are the achievement.

Execute with initiative and seek innovation.

Count accountability as your responsibility to yourself and others.

Taste the hunger for what feeds you and drives you to the next level.

Ann had me as a mentor to assist. I suggest to everyone to always seek mentors, and as they grow, pay it forward and mentor others. However, having mentors or the assistance of others through this exercise is important. I recommend choosing only those that the individual's trust, and perhaps someone that can do the exercise simultaneously. This will allow each to dive deep and bring out the best results and commitments from all participants.

Create A Personal Mission Statement:

Much like for an organization, a mission statement is your personal reason for existence, your purpose. When defined and embraced, the mission statement should act as a guide to decisions and direction for your life. By understanding and believing in your individual mission statement, this should guide you on employment choices, as well as other choices in your life and career. Does your purpose match where you work, where you contribute and what you believe in? Also, once defining your personal mission statement, this should allow your accountability partners to hold

· · · · · · · · · · ·

The mission statement should act as a guide to decisions and direction for your life.

· · · · · · · · · · ·

you accountable, which will help keep your commitment to your mission. A mission statement is external, your purpose to yourself and others. It's your purpose in life as well. Later, we will discuss a vision statement, which is more internal and defines your three to five-year plan with large goals that drive you. In simple terms, your mission statement defines what is important to you. Sometimes in life we reach a crossroads where a decision needs to be made. Your mission statement should be your guide.

Steven Covey explains a mission statement as *"connecting with your unique purpose and the profound satisfaction that comes from fulfilling it."*

The exercise we completed on values and principles helped build the framework that is the foundation of your individual mission statement, and there should be no conflict. With Ann, we kept her Principle Statements within our view to ensure they aligned. We started with the question to Ann, what is important to her, and how can her successes in the past demonstrate this? Also, we asked what disappointments and failures occurred that diminished what she believed in or what was important to her. Although sometimes painful, the exercise allowed Ann to see her successes, as well as disappointments, and the reasons for each. Ann recognized that the successes occurred with her focus on the right belief that drove her mission, although not defined at the time. However, where she faced failure and disappointment, she realized that when obstacles occurred she had no guide to give correctional direction and this contributed to the failure. The next stage for Ann was to think big picture and envision if she had the ability to pay it forward in society, what would she do? We also looked at some of the things she did in the past and asked if budget and time were not an issue, how would that have changed. Ann believed in empowering other women, especially those that had suffered abuse. She helped single mothers and families in need. She was very committed to the experience that impover-ished children had as it was important to her that they see life with big dreams and high expectations. This exercise allowed me as a mentor to see special aspects of Ann, to coach her more and it allowed her to see that she had tremendous value to society. With this perspective we challenged her to draft a few sample mission statements to choose from that defined her.

Ann's Mission Statement:

To seek solutions and betterment of myself and others through compassion and effort, and to face the future with an optimistic outlook.

We added this mission statement to the Principle Statement document banner we created for Ann. The mission statement gave Ann guidance in her decisions and a direction she chose for herself in life. This also allowed her to assess if her current employer was a fit. Fortunately, since I was her mentor demonstrating we saw value in her, she defined we were the right employer at this time. But this is what a personal mission statement should do. It should drive all your decisions, relationships, employment and even purchases. Much like the values and principles, they all act as a guide.

Evaluate your gifts and abilities:

To further take the steps on defining what you will live by, the next stage is to evaluate your gifts and abilities. What are the traits that you have that can be enhanced to build you into a great leader? What are your strengths and weaknesses? How do others view you, both your peers and superiors? Are there certain traits, that with improvement, will get you recognized as a future leader? These are all questions to define in this stage, with humility, as it is important that if even painful we identify your strengths and weaknesses. In the book *Strength-Based Leadership* by Tom Rath, and the follow-up *Strength Finder* that was co-written with Barry Conchie, they provide an assessment that helps define one's strengths. I like assessments, whether online or those executed on paper. Both have their reasons for effectiveness. The paper assessments, when utilized to have peers rate you, allow a simple process for evaluation. The online assessment helps you recognize with a systematic evaluation, by answering questions, your strengths and weaknesses. These are separate ways of testing what your personal assessment shows as value. My mother would always teach me that humility, as a leader, is a strength. She stated this because she wanted me to recognize openly how others viewed me. If I viewed it with a lack of humility, I would think of reasons why their views were not accurate. With humility, I would take a step back and evaluate what they view, how they view it and why they view it that way. Humility would also teach me to appreciate such feedback and not be apprehensive about it. With Ann, we took this next step.

Ann and I created a quick list of leadership traits and characteristics and listed them in a spreadsheet. There are great resources to determine which traits you find value in. We created a list and it is the same one I utilize in coaching today. We then simply listed three quick choices: 1. Needs Improvement, 2. Meets Standard, 3. Exceeds. Between each trait we created a space for any comments, as comments were both welcomed and sought after. Ann created a list, with my mentorship, on those peers who could give good insight from first-hand knowledge and interaction about her. We additionally defined individuals outside of her department, that through departmental needs, interacted with her on the job and would give good insight from their point of view and perception. Finally, we listed a few superiors, one she directly reported to, as well as others she interacted with. We approached them via email and communicated the purpose of the evaluation. We emphasized the importance of their honest feedback, as well as the need to be as direct as possible. We explained in the email communication how their information was going to allow us to create goals and development plans for Ann's future. So any lack of honesty would short change the process and Ann's development. We sent the evaluation to each participant and requested that they execute the assessment and send it back to me within 24-hours. I monitored each reply and assessment returned. Then I sent a reminder to any still outstanding on the morning of the requested scheduled return date.

Mark Villareal
People, Strategy, Execution

Leadership Traits Evaluation

Please evaluate the leader listed based upon the following criteria:
1. Needs Improvement   2. Meets Standards   3. Exceeds Standards

In addition, please evaluate with high expectations of leadership. Please leave an explanation for any score of 1. Needs Improvement, for the individual being evaluated to gain insight for development.

Exceeds Standards should be rare, and must have a comment with an example on why you scored in that manner.

Trait   1. Needs Improvement   2. Meets Standards   3. Exceeds Standards

1 *Vision*   ☐   ☐   ☐
The leader shares the vision constantly, clearly and points to small victories and progress.
Comment: _____

2 *Communication* ☐   ☐   ☐
The leader must communicate constantly and effectively. Addressing important issues quickly.
Comment: _____

3 *Decisiveness* ☐   ☐   ☐
A leader must be decisive, yet with wisdom based upon sound facts. Decisions are made timely with confidence.
Comment: _____

4 *Integrity/Honesty* ☐   ☐   ☐
The leader demonstrates and has earned trust through integrity and shows transparency.
Comment: _____

5 *Inspiration*   ☐   ☐   ☐
A leader must inspire and gain followers through belief in their leadership of others.
Comment: _____

6 *Optimism*   ☐   ☐   ☐
Leaders must have the ability to instill optimism to those that follow as well as to peers and superiors.
Comment: _____

7 *Facilitation* ☐ ☐ ☐
The leader has a strong ability to lead and facilitate their team and others to focus on goal achievement.
Comment: _____

8 *Commitment* ☐ ☐ ☐
The leader demonstrates genuine commitment and passion that followers, peers and superiors believe in.
Comment: _____

9 *Accountability* ☐ ☐ ☐
The leader accepts accountability and holds others accountable for high standards and achievement.
Comment: _____

10 *Empowerment* ☐ ☐ ☐
The leader defines parameters that empower and develops others to take action and make decisions.
Comment: _____

11 *Creativity* ☐ ☐ ☐
The leader has shown creativity and innovation for new ideas and embraces the same from their team.
Comment: _____

12 *Empathy* ☐ ☐ ☐
The leader demonstrates a strong understanding of each individual. This is a strong grasp of emotional intelligence.
Comment: _____

Additional Comments & Feedback: _____

_____

_____

_____

_____

_____

_____

As the assessments were sent out, it was important to have Ann assess herself before viewing any responses or opinions. Self-assessments can go either way, as some individuals may tend to be harder on themselves. However, there are those that may grade themselves higher than they truly are. This can cause a concern as defining areas of improvement is essential for development and lacking reality may hinder that development.

The first thing Ann and I did was review each trait so she would have a clear understanding on each. This also allowed me to probe with questioning and for Ann to describe examples from her personal experiences in her employment history, as well as in everyday life. Ann and I went trait by trait discussing each in turn. The first trait was vision. I explained that vision from a leader is extremely important. Vision is how a leader helps their people believe and stay focused on the goal. A leader with great vision has a team that knows the target, understands where they are and has a plan for that achievement. I described to Ann some great leaders that I had in the past, who always communicated small wins, which allowed their team to believe by envisioning they were making progress. I explained that a leader's vision is more than

* * * * * * * * * * *

Vision is a belief in success and achievement, long term.

* * * * * * * * * * *

about the Vision Statement of the organization, as that is part of it, but a Vision Statement is a 3 to 5 year outlook, with a big, hairy, audacious goal. So even with a vision statement, a strong leader will point to small wins and communicate to the team where they stand. But vision as a whole, is a belief in success and achievement, long term.

So I asked Ann about examples with her and vision. She struggled at first in defining an example in her current role. I asked her about raising her son, who was then age twelve. I asked how she instills and impacts his outlook of life, his goals and dreams and his perception of his future. Her eyes lit up as her son means everything to her. She spoke about how she encourages him first to do well in school and they also would have discussions why that is important and how it relates to opportunity with colleges in the future. When I pressed further in what has helped him in getting good grades, she mentioned that she had worked with him to develop good habits. I complemented her as that is exactly good leadership. It starts with small things and habits to help create success or failure. Ann recognized this as being important, and having an effect on her son to develop good habits was a great demonstration of instilling vision. Her son believed what she instilled and formed good habits with her guidance. We then discussed her son's goals and she described how he wanted to study chemical engineering, and how this had driven his focus to do well in math and science. I was impressed that her son had such a hefty goal and already understood that with that goal how math and science would play an important role. He worked hard for solid grades in these areas. Ann was doing a good job while creating and instilling vision within her son. She understood the aspect of vision by a leader much clearer.

Next we discussed her level with vision, within her current role. Ann had great examples, but understood that in her role as an admin there was a larger opportunity for growth. We did discuss what she could do within her role to expand on vision. How she could assist those she reports to in having information in small and large victories. How she can gain an understanding on vision that is important to that leader and how she can play a role. There is a great adage that states that if you want to grow into a leader, help your leader grow. The experience alone adds value. So with this discussion, Ann rated herself a #1 - Needs Improvement. She stated in the comments section to herself to look for opportunities in helping her superiors and to recognize small victories. This was an important step for her to understand as some individuals believe they cannot grow in the vision area until they are a leader. Committing to learn, engage and getting involved is a great way to develop, grow, and gain opportunities in being mentored and to obtain recognition.

The next trait for Ann and I to discuss was communication. Within the trait definition, it states that the leader must communicate constantly and effectively, as well as address important issues quickly. The last part is an important part as I explained to Ann that weak leaders will sometimes avoid difficult issues, and this can cause problems. Then I asked about other leaders she had seen and admired, and what stood out about how they communicated. Her first statement was that they never let up communicating. They would tell stories and break things down in different ways. She stated that the best ones repeated themselves in a way that you understood what was important to them. She further emphasized that the leaders were able to break things down differently to individuals at different levels. So Ann, with this exercise, understood that communication in a broader sense was ensuring the team members were informed and understood from communication designed for them. I personally am a leader who repeats himself constantly. The book *The Rockefeller Habits* has a statement that says, "Until your people start mocking you, you have not said your message enough."

Once again, Ann and I had a discussion about her current role, and her personal role at home. In her current role as an admin, she did have to communicate effectively and constantly as she was the go between for her supervisor and the team she was servicing. Ann had to follow up with the leader she reported to, be well informed and comprehend what that leader needed. She had to, at times, express this to others to gain results and follow through. She realized, as we discussed how she has understood the differences in the employees she interacts with, and with this understanding she knows how to alter her communication for effectiveness. Ann also laughed, as at home her son complains that she repeats herself constantly. Yet, he has acknowledged that those items where she repeats her message, has taught him to remember her message clearer and this has allowed him to have good instincts. So Ann rated herself #2 - Meets Standards in this category. She wrote in her comments to find ways to challenge herself in understanding additional effective ways of communication. She stated she wanted to develop in the area of storytelling, which strong leaders do well.

* * * * * * * * * * *

A molder of consensus will gain insight and opinions, but will make the decisions they believe best for the organization.

* * * * * * * * * * *

Decisiveness was the next trait for us to work with. From experience, I get frustrated with a leader who cannot make a decision. However, some leaders try to make decisions by committee, which is also a sign of a weak manager. Certainly a manager should gain insight from others, but Martin Luther King Jr. stated that a true leader is "a molder of consensus", not a builder. A manager that makes decisions by committee is a builder of consensus. A molder of consensus will gain insight and opinions, but will make the decisions they believe best for the organization. From that point they have built their team to understand that their opinions added value, but if the decision is different than what they stated, as a team member, they need to embrace it and own it as their own. The leader who made the decision will now effectively work with the team, communicate the plan and gain everyone's commitment and effort. We discussed that an important factor of a strong leader who is decisive also has a process that allows them to make solid decisions based upon factors known, as well as educated assumptions. Smart decisions and bad decisions can take the same amount of time. Strong leaders will even take risks. But that risk is a calculated risk, not a blind risk. Ann really absorbed the conversation and asked great questions.

Ann was able to quickly produce examples where she had to make decisions for the manager she worked for on things she was assigned to follow up on. She realized that because she was kept well informed that she believed her decisions were good decisions based upon good information. She enjoyed knowing that her manager always appreciated that she made a decision, so that the employees were never left hanging. At times, he would coach her on different aspects she may have considered in the decision, and this helped her to develop better decision making skills. Ann had a pretty good grasp in this area and realized that as a parent most decisions were based upon being safe, staying fed and being financially responsible. She rated herself a #2 - Meets Standards in this category. In her comments she stated she would take a couple courses on effective decision making and problem solving to advance in this area.

Integrity and honesty were the next traits on the list. The definition defined on the evaluation is that the leader demonstrates and has earned trust through integrity and shows transparency. As Ann and I discussed, she asked me to define the transparency portion of the definition. I explained that strong leaders show transparency and utilize it as a tool to grow others. They communicate the thought process behind decisions and are also quick to correct individuals with honest feedback. These leaders believe that they owe this to those they are leading and even explain it as such. This allows them to have frank and direct discussions that are constructive and professional, as well as appreciated. Integrity and honesty to most of us would be self-explanatory. However, Ann brought up a past employer experience that she had where the manager seemed to have convenient memory lapses. Certainly we all may forget a thing or two, but when it becomes a pattern it clearly sends a warning signal. Especially when the convenient memory lapse favors a situation that would be different if what was committed to was remembered. Ann stated the employees lost trust in that manager. So trust and integrity is something that is seen over time by ones actions. Someone can easily state they can be trusted, but actions will define if that is true or not.

When Ann and I talked about trust and integrity, she quickly discussed how important is was for her son to understand. She, at times, was concerned about the adult examples around him and what a child picks up in observation. This is a powerful thing, as in business if you cross the ethics line as a leader, how can you get angry at others that do the same? Trust and integrity is a standard to set and live. She explained that once her son came home from a weekend trip he took with his friend's family. He had a cell phone he wanted to access, but needed the password. She immediately inquired on where he got the phone from. Her son explained that someone left it on a park bench and forgot it. After he observed it for some time, and believed they were not coming back for it, he then took it for himself. His logic was that once they lost the phone that it was okay for him to take, as this was the standard he learned from friends. Ann took time to explain to her son that if it was not his to begin with, that it does not matter if someone else lost it. It is not his property. She wanted to instill integrity as a principle in her son so it would be automatic within his mind. Ann had a good grasp on the subject and we even discussed examples in her role where some team members that she services may have asked her for work favors that crossed the line, or were definitely in the gray area. Ann would have access to the employee time clock and some would ask her to make changes, which she would not do. In other instances, they would ask her to fudge a number or not report something to management. Ann demonstrated integrity and honesty as a principle consistently so that soon the requests diminished.

Ann rated herself #2 - Meets Standards. She discussed with me the possibility of rating herself a #3 - Exceeds, which others might agree with. However, here is where I coached her on why #3 - Exceeds are rare. The first question was to ask her, "Should not any leader meet standards of high integrity and honesty?" We should have high standards on integrity and honesty and set that qualification as meeting standards. Ann asked what then would possibly be an 'exceeds' in this area? I explained a few scenarios that I have witnessed over the years where the leader brought forth information that although damaging to them obtaining a goal, or a company objective, their integrity still made them bring it forward. Ann understood, and rated herself a #2 - Meets Standards, and with my recommendation, she wrote in her comments to read the book *The Speed Of Trust* and to expand her understanding of integrity and honesty as a leader.

We next moved on to the trait of inspiration. This is defined as a leader must inspire and gain followers in belief of their leadership of others. I equate this to great coaches. Ann is a Dallas Cowboy fan, as well as a sports fan in general. We spoke about how great coaches inspire their team to not only follow, but to raise their expectations and effort. By observation, you can see the team have more motivation and belief. In many instances, sometimes that coach is even more demanding and pressing. I once read a story where Emmitt Smith, the Hall of Fame running back, asked Jimmy Johnson, his coach, why he was so tough on him? Johnson answered back that as every player witnessed him being tough on Smith, a player with great dedication and work ethic, then each player knew their standards and efforts must be elevated. Smith understood and welcomed the role from that point forward. To inspire individuals is to create a fire within them with a desire to improve and grow. Inspiration does go with sharing the vision, and truly creates the environment where each person works towards its achievement. When employees are inspired they appreciate their employer and leader and they want the organization to have success.

Ann spoke about herself, as she admitted that when she applied for her current role it was with the mindset to work in that role forever. It was the environment within our workplace that encouraged her to have a larger view of herself. Perhaps she had been beaten down by others, which happens many times in relationships and friendships. She always knew she had good abilities and has done well at several jobs. But now she had been encouraged to take the steps in developing those further and to have aspirations to grow into leadership. At home, she encourages and inspires her son which has had a strong effect on his goals and objectives. In what we discussed, and having met her son, I believe she has done a solid job. So for inspiration, she rated herself a #2 - Meets Standards. With my mentorship, she placed in the comment section to read *The One Minute Manager*, which as I explained is a book that changed my life.

Optimism was the next trait, with the definition being that a leader must have the ability to instill optimism to those that follow and to peers as well as superiors. So it is much more than just having an optimistic view. Much like inspiration, great leaders exhibit optimism that becomes infectious to others and they feed off that optimism. This is also why I recommend the book *The One Minute Manager* as it teaches to help someone grow

> *Great leaders exhibit optimism that becomes infectious to others and they feed off that optimism.*

by catching them doing something right. This inspires them and it helps build an optimistic belief when they are encouraged consistently with tangible recognition and coaching of accomplishments. The leader must demonstrate that with their optimism is a realistic outlook with results. Consistent performance is essential as this helps build a track record of performance where that leader's optimism is seen with validity. This is where not only employees, but also peers and superiors, are optimistic on that leader's insight. However, a leader can lose confidence if they always have an optimistic viewpoint, but their results lack consistency, so there is a balance to optimism.

Ann appreciated that her direct supervisor instilled inspiration and grew optimism by his belief in her and others. She had seen and had been the beneficiary of his optimistic insight and had even seen him display optimism when something was not achieved. However, he was optimistic as he believed proper effort was given, and they just missed the mark. He encouraged and coached the team to success the second go around. Ann understood how optimism has opened her eyes on what she can achieve. She also has been known to echo her supervisor's comments to the team members when pushing for achievement, or when needing encouragement. She has earned the reputation as a cheerleader, which is an unexpected value from an admin. Together we rated her #2 - Meets Standards. In her comments she stated that she would start each day by asking herself and the team, how she could assist in their success? Ann was working on establishing a leader's mindset, which impressed me.

Facilitation was the next trait listed. The definition given for facilitation is that the leader has a strong ability to lead and facilitate their team and others to focus on goal achievement. Most individuals when they hear the word facilitation think of a person who conducts workshops and meetings. Yes, they facilitate those events. But as I discussed with Ann, facilitation skills are something used by someone who can guide and direct others with the skill of allowing them to come to a proper conclusion with them by taking them through the process. The skill allows the individuals being taught to learn while executing and to draw their own conclusion. However, the facilitator has the skill to help direct them to what is determined as being the right conclusion. Now because we are speaking about leadership, the predetermined conclusion would not sacrifice any proper values or principles. Ann grasped this concept and understood quickly. She replied with two examples of when her immediate supervisor had worked with her and some team members, and even allowed and assigned them some research. She knows that her manager could have just educated them on the conclusion, but by facilitating them through the process they each learned better problem solving skills which was the intent of her manager. She appreciated this.

Ann spoke about her father and mother and how parents have natural facilitation skills. She spoke about the value of facilitation in helping her son come to his own conclusions. This skill has tremendous value even when her son had made a bad decision and faced the consequences. Facilitation was valuable because before the process, her son would be disappointed that he was caught more than he would because he did something wrong. She has been able to facilitate that whether he was caught or not, that it was a bad decision. In addition, not being caught would allow him to develop bad habits, and to make more bad decisions. Ann realized that although she utilized this skill some at home and a little at the office, she had great room for development on this trait. She rated herself a #1. - Needs Improvement. In her comments section she wrote that she would add to her development plan. Perhaps even take an online course.

Commitment and passion were the next traits. They are listed together as they are good traits to be measured as one. The leader demonstrates genuine commitment and passion that followers, peers and superiors believe in. This is how these traits are listed on the evaluation. I asked Ann to describe how she has witnessed this and she described two items. One, she realizes that her immediate supervisor continues to demonstrate his commitment to his team. When he states he will follow through, he does. But because he does stand on his commitment she sees that he asks more of others, and he does so with a passion for completion that brings better results. He rallies the team and each member believes in his leadership because of his passion and commitment.

> *The leader demonstrates genuine commitment and passion that followers, peers and superiors believe in.*

Next she complimented me, which was a nice gesture. She stated that my commitment to her development surprised her, as she sees that it is nothing that I have to do, yet she appreciates it. She said that near the beginning she may have wanted to stop the sessions, but my commitment and belief in her pushed her to continue. She stated that my passion in her development has helped her believe in herself more and has raised her level of expectations of herself. When we discussed her, I had to state that those she serves appreciate her as she is an admin that serves them with commitment and passion. I have heard how she stays on top of them when it comes to projects, deadlines and numbers for them to achieve and do better for themselves. She shows a commitment and passion for the business as a whole, and has participated and led some of our community involvement committees and projects. She had not realized that her passion and commitment were that visible, yet admitted that is how she feels. She rated herself a #2 - Meets Standards, but wrote in her comments a commitment to keep her level high as she develops to future positions.

Moving to the next trait, accountability was on the list. The leader holds themselves, and others, accountable to high standards and achievement. This is how it was listed on the evaluation. Obviously accountability is a word tossed around and it is good that we truly evaluate the word with the person. The first thing with accountability is the question, does the person hold themselves accountable? Too many who want to be leaders believe or demonstrate their will on others in showing everyone they have authority to hold them accountable. This is not leadership when done this way. True leaders first demonstrate with humility and a passion that self-accountability is important to them. They admit when they miss the mark and show more determination to get it right. By demonstrating this they gain followers because their self-accountability is infectious. By being genuine and demonstrating that accountability is for the achievement of the objective, whether individual or broad, it is for the benefit of all. So implementing accountability to others is understood, accepted and many times welcomed. An effective leader can motivate with accountability with proper measures and an accountability plan.

Ann picked up on this right away. She liked how her immediate supervisor demonstrated self-accountability, and many times shared methods he utilized with the team that educated them on self-accountability. She said that he did it in such a way that helped them learn the importance of self-accountability and how it helped drive his success. She had embraced the same methods and demonstrated to the team in the same manner. Each team member knew that Ann always wanted to be timely and accurate on projects and they witnessed the method she utilized to be accountable. She had taught, and continues to teach, her son in the same manner. She worked for a supervisor whose team then understood account-ability and they are held to a high standard of accountability. However, because her supervisor had instilled self-accountability so well, overall accountability is easier. Ann rated herself #2 - Meets Standards on accountability. In her comments I recommended she explore the book *The Rockefeller Habits* by Verne Harnish.

Empowerment was next on the list of traits on the evaluation. The leader defines parameters that empowers and develops others to take action and make decisions. This was the definition given on the evaluation form. Ann asked for more clarity on this defini-tion. I explained that empowerment is the art and skill to build an environment where team players understand their role and respon-sibility. However, true empowerment is when they comprehend the direction and objectives of the organization, and where they can own their own portion and take initiative when presented with an opportunity to push that objective forward. The leader must educate on goals and objectives, and where mission, vision and values play a large role. Smart leaders then create, communicate and educate the parameters for their team, while teaching them to make decisions within those parameters. Leaders who do not empower their team create an environment where the team lacks initiative and waits on the leader. I further gave Ann some exam-ples on how I encourage my team to make decisions and show appreciation when they do. I teach my team that I may coach them on their decision to further advance their decision-making process. But as long as it is within the defined parameters given, they need to make decisions. Then I gave a more specific example on an employee going over and above for a client as they needed to correct a situation. Their solution cost our organization minimal and they satisfied the client. When I worked with that employee on their decision-making process they determined the problem was real and our fault. He then stated that one of our principle statements was to always do right by the client. So they made a decision to correct the situation. I was pleased with the decision and their process. Had the solution been costly that employee would have sought our advice, but since it was minimal they took initiative and made the decision.

Ann appreciated the breakdown. We spoke about how she empowers her son to think for himself and make decisions. She also emphasized that she teaches him to not only make decisions, but to own them. She made a great point. Great leaders teach their team to take initiative and expect accountability. This is what she was teaching her son and it was a testament to her logic that she understood the importance. Ann next spoke on how her supervisor empowers her by pushing and coaching her on decision-making. She was asked to train a few other admins hired for other departments. She also had to empower them in order to ensure they were the most effective. She believed an admin must be aggressive in finding ways to help their team. The more they help, the better the team can focus on results. With this understanding, Ann rated herself a #2 - Meets Standards. In the comments she wrote to look for more ways to empower others and to seek empowerment. Those that seek empowerment will catapult their growth.

Creativity and Innovation were two traits listed together and they were defined as: the leader has shown creativity and innovation for new ideas and embraces the same from their team. I asked Ann to define this for me. She stated that she believed that this is where leaders think outside the box, which she appreciates about her supervisor. Ann had observed that her supervisor would look for alternative solutions and also be open to ideas for ways to improve a better process. In other words her supervisor would demonstrate that he was creative and innovative, and he welcomed that from others. She did see where there is a balance, as she had witnessed times where he pushed back since creativity and innovation does not mean let's change everything. Many times he would ask about what is wrong with the present way? Sometimes what is in the box is fine. Her supervisor would state the measurement is improvement, without taking a shortcut. Taking shortcuts may make a solution quicker, but may cause harm at some point because a process was missed or eliminated.

Ann had a good grasp on this trait. I actually brought up some solutions that Ann herself created and brought to our attention. This is part of the reason I started mentoring her, as her creativity and innovation helped her get noticed. Ann took our standard reports and built new ones that interlocked while providing additional and valuable information. She took initiative on her own with this report. On another item she created a daily task for the team she served for them to complete and report each day. Management was unaware, but when supplied with the results and data they were both surprised and impressed. Here is where Ann gave herself a #2 - Meets Standards. Although here I would have allowed a #3 based upon her admin role, but #2 fits for a leadership role. Ann stated in her comments to always look for ways to be innovative. As she advances I could recommend books to read, like *Blue Ocean Strategy*, but that will come as she is in leadership for a while.

Empathy was the final trait in the evaluation form. The definition listed stated that a leader demonstrates strong understanding of each individual. This is a foundation of emotional intelligence. Emotional intelligence is a trait that advanced leaders have strong skills in. So having and demonstrating empathy as an aspiring and beginning leader is important as a foundation to build the skill forward. Empathy is the ability to place yourself in another person's situation and understand how it feels. Empathy allows one the ability to understand and be sensitive to the thoughts, feelings and the experience one encounters. This trait then allows that leader to address situations with that empathy in mind. They may address the situation differently and take a different tactic between employees.

Ann went directly to thoughts of her son. She had experienced and witnessed times when he came across a disappointment, and she remembered how it felt to her when she was that age. This allowed her to have a conversation with that in mind. It further allowed her to listen intently, remember the feeling and then address her advice with the knowledge of what may come next. As a youth, things may be more amplified. As an adult we may be prone to come across as not understanding, because as an adult we may view it as petty. Ann recognized this as a mother and it had given her the gift of empathy.

> *Empathy is the ability to place yourself in another person's situation and understand how it feels.*

Ann further described how she interacted with the employees she served differently based upon their personalities and needs. This is the start of understanding emotional intelligence which is a good sign. Ann rated herself a #2 - Meets Expectations and wrote within her comment section to search for additional resources to advance her empathy into stronger emotional intelligence.

You can see how this exercise, especially with a mentor or trusted advisor, is important. Ann was educated on each item. She had the ability to describe each in her own terms, both at work and at home, which adds value. Ann was able to imagine herself growing and could see herself as a future leader. Visualizing is the first step of any dream. To make a dream a reality will take planning, a roadmap, effort and achievement. Now the next part was to review the evaluations submitted by those asked to execute. As these evaluations were sent back, I separated them based upon role. Ann's peers I placed together, while any from superiors and management I kept separate. This would allow us to review them from a position mindset. Some of the things you look for when reviewing is important feedback, as sometimes your best suggestions come from evaluations. Next you look for scoring consistency as well as inconsistency. Is there a trait or two where others show they view Ann differently, that is consistent among the respondents? Or is it just one respondent? Are people evaluating the subject at a higher level than the person themselves? This is not uncommon as individuals who are striving for development tend to be harder on themselves. The important part is to review each returned evaluation with an open mind. In addition, I counseled Ann not to try to guess on who did the evaluation, although I know human nature takes over.

Ann and I met and she seemed a little nervous. I understand, that finding how others may rate and define you can make you a little nervous. However, to me, it is a good sign that Ann is nervous, as it shows she wants to be viewed in a good light. This is an indicator of humility, which is an important value in a leader. Humility is an indicator of a servant's heart. Servant Leadership is the leadership I believe in, as it builds a long and lasting culture. Ann and I started with the evaluation from the peers first.

As we started reading, the first impression was each evaluation was really close to what Ann had evaluated on herself. A good sign was that many left comments in an attempt to be helpful. This is a good sign of respect. Although sometimes participants will leave comments not too flattering, that is usually for someone who has been a manager for a while that may truly lack leadership. In this scenario, they know Ann's aspirations and the feedback was a sign that they want to help her succeed. That was my first message to Ann. Most agreed with Ann on Vision, #1 - Needs Improvement. Although the comments showed support that Ann understands vision in their opinion, she just needs to be comfortable sharing the vision from her role. They encouraged her to share it, as they stated that Ann tended to be well informed of the goals and objectives, as well as the roadblocks. This allowed me to express to Ann to not be afraid to step outside her comfort zone and share the vision along with her superiors. This demonstrates that you don't have to be in management to be a leader, while having those that will follow.

Communication was one where they agreed that she meets expectations. But the comments added value as some stated that the reports she has created really has helped them, and they appreciate her email communication and reminders. Another comment was that she was consistent in her messaging. On Decisiveness they also rated her a #2 - Meets Standards and a couple of comments stated that she seems to be in sync with her superior. So if they know he is away, they appreciate that they can go to her and that she makes decisions. One comment stated that they were surprised at first that she was not afraid to make decisions and own them. They truly appreciated that about her. I mentored Ann that this was good feedback and whether she knew it before, when she steps out with confidence others see her leadership traits.

For Integrity and Honesty they rated Ann #2 - Meets Standards with a couple evaluations rating her #3 - Exceeds Standards. This was no surprise, but some of the comments stated Ann truly stands on integrity on the rules and for the benefit of the company. On one of the #3 ratings, they stated that it is evident that Ann holds herself to high standards and that her integrity was non-negotiable. This means integrity has become a principle for Ann, as it is automatic. That was a great sign. For Inspiration and Optimism, their ratings were #2 - Meets Standards, but the comments almost made it look like some wanted to give her a #3 - Exceeds. They spoke about how she encourages them and how they are surprised by her knowledge of their objectives. One stated that they seek her advice as she has earned respect for her knowledge. So far the responses had been encouraging. But through the process, I had Ann add some of the feedback to her overall review that she did, so she can review them at one spot.

Facilitation was one where the evaluations were split, as a few gave her #1 - Needs Improvement, which is also what Ann rated herself. However, a few gave her #2 - Meets Standards and the comments mentioned that she prepared for group meetings well, taking the lead and burden off of management. This was good feedback for Ann and it allowed us to see how what we may believe are small actions are noticed by others. However, Commitment and Passion were solid #2 - Meets Standards with high comments on how she encourages them with her work ethic, commitment to get things done timely and the passion for individuals achieving their goals and objectives. A few stated they were surprised how well she knew the goals of the individuals. I emphasized to Ann to keep building on that passion and commitment, as these are two indicators of a servant leader. Which is what I preach. The difference to me between a manager and a servant leader is a distance of 12 inches. This means the difference is the distance from their mind and their heart. A manager knows the rules and leads with his mind. A servant leader knows the same, but has instilled them in their heart.

On Accountability, several actually rated her #3 - Exceeds Standards, and the others at #2 - Meets Standards. They overwhelmingly commented that she holds herself accountable which allows her to hold the team accountable. One jokingly commented that you cannot fool her, offer excuses or claim ignorance. With Empowerment they all rated her #2 - Meets Standards, stating that she does a good job with communicating expectations and processes so that they are well informed and that allows them to make decisions. I asked Ann her thoughts on their comments. She seemed a little embarrassed, which is the humility within her. But she stated how the statements reaffirmed what she was doing. This validated her beliefs that she had been hesitant and unsure on. With validation she would confidently pursue consistently, as well as start trusting her instincts.

Creativity and Innovation received consistent #2 - Meet Standards, but the comments did recognize the reports she had created that provided solid information for the team. They saw her value in how she was trying to proactively serve them. A few comments actually pushed and suggested ways she can step out on creativity and innovation more. Some recommended she work a little more directly with a team member or two to learn additional parts of the business and expand on this trait further. This is one suggestion we would share with her superior. On Empathy, all rated her a #2 - Meets Standards, but some comments stated she might be too empathetic or she may be confusing empathy with sympathy, which may allow some to take advantage of her. This was appreciated feedback as it demonstrates a respect for Ann to provide this insight to be aware on how she can become a stronger leader.

Ann and I then spoke to this process and how it had affected her. She stated it was tremendous as she had done what is natural to her, or what she refers to as common sense. The feedback validated that she was moving in the right direction which now gave her confidence. We reviewed again the overall comments, trait by trait, to make any necessary notes. This is a solid exercise that by doing a 360 evaluation we have a foundation that can be implemented into a development plan when we arrive at that stage with Ann. Now it was time for Ann and me to review the three evaluations from superiors to understand their rating and feedback. This is usually a quicker process unless there is a large discrepancy in the evaluation. Superiors tend to be a little more direct, yet complimentary, if a good candidate is being evaluated.

As Ann and I reviewed the evaluations we did not come across any large discrepancies. What we did find was great feedback on comments, as superiors have been through the process before and tend to provide good recommendations and feedback. Each were united that Ann was a solid prospect for leadership and that her abilities were far greater than her role. The most valuable feedback was that each superior had great resources to suggest. One recommended some leadership courses through Dale Carnegie and had a partnership where our investment would be reasonable. Others suggested some online courses, as well as books. Once again this gave a solid foundation for a development plan that will be built from this foundation. The key to this exercise is not only building a foundation of what you will live by, which gives guidance, but it allows the prospect to gain a better commitment. I once heard a person state that confidence is overrated, but that was just a foolish sales pitch. Confidence is a key foundational emotion that helps push someone forward. Lack of confidence will always allow doubt, but strong self-confidence will build courage.

As the person aspiring to be a leader, it is important to create a template that showcases what you will live by. We recommend, as stated, that you create a flyer that you post that demonstrates your personal Mission Statement, as well

. . . .

Lack of confidence will always allow doubt, but strong self-confidence will build courage.

. . . .

as your Principle Statements. Read them daily. When faced with a decision, take a moment to evaluate every decision to ensure they match each. Soon this will become automatic. Then take your self-evaluation along with the notes from peers and superiors and create a spreadsheet on each trait and outline some commitments with timelines and measures so you can hold yourself accountable.

Share with your mentor and gain their feedback. Make adjustments if necessary. Take a moment at the end of each day and ask yourself if what you did today advanced any of those traits. You will find days where nothing you did advanced the traits and here is where you have to assess why. We allow ourselves to get caught up with tasks and lose focus. As we move forward with the next steps, we will speak of tools that will help implement focus and accountability.

Chapter 2

DEFINE WHAT YOU
WILL LIVE FOR

Chapter One was where we discussed what you will live by, which guides your decisions and builds the foundation in which you will build upon. Chapter Two is a one-word difference. Define what you will live for now defines the direction you take upon that foundation. How you structure the roadmaps to your success is important, and that roadmap needs to know what you are reaching for. What is it that you are trying to achieve? What are your goals and objectives? What will assist you in ensuring that you will have the tools and the skills to achieve what you will live for? This is your ultimate purpose, and to build it properly one needs to structure a plan for success and not a failure. However, setbacks happen, and how you prepare for adjustments is essential. Failure is a part of learning and also a part of effort and courage. Taking risks and going after what you desire is not easy. But then again, that is why you must define what you will live for.

In Chapter One we discussed values and principles, as they are the very core of living inside out. Living inside out defines that your values are so ingrained within, not only in your mind but also within your heart. They are at the core of who you are. So as you make decisions, and as people learn about who you are, they will make their perceptions based upon your actions. That is the outside part of inside out and they display who you are. Upon that foundation you then developed your personal Mission Statement, which defines and announces your purpose in life. Your mission is your reason for existence, as well as what drives and guides you. Your values, principles and mission guide you every moment and every day. They are the guide for every decision. But now it is time to define what they are guiding you to? They are pushing you in a direction. But what are you reaching for? That is what you will live for. The essence of what is your vision of the next 3 to 5 years. What do you wish to achieve and what is your plan? What are your goals and objectives? What do you have to develop about you, with your skills and knowledge, to achieve what you will live for?

Create your personal Vision Statement:

Remember, a Mission Statement is external. It defines your purpose and reason for existence for everyone to see. It, along with your values and principles, guide you. Your personal Vision Statement is internal. This should be what drives you and provides focus. Remember, it is what you will live for! What are you being driven to? Why is that so important? What will that mean if you obtain it? How will your life change, develop, or take on more meaning? A personal Vision Statement needs to provide focus as well as a large challenge. In 3 to 5 years where would you want to be? We teach that you define that vision while striving for more. This is what we call adding a BHAG. What is a BHAG? A BHAG is a

Big Hairy Audacious Goal.[1] Something that makes you reach and stretch beyond your abilities to achieve. Something that drives you daily, scares you at times and focuses you for achievement. What is your big hairy audacious goal? Do you know?

Develop Foundational Core Goals:

Working with Ann, we took the next steps by executing some exercises that would provide information of what is important. So the first part I challenged Ann to think of goals for some key areas of her life. What is her outlook for these key areas in the next 3 to 5 years, and why do those goals have any importance to her? What are their meaning? I call these Foundational Core Goals. I handed her a worksheet to fill in her answers.

---

1 Jim Collins and Jerry Porras, *Built To Last: Successful Habits Of Visionary Companies*

Mark Villareal

People, Strategy, Execution

Foundational Core Goals

Define goals and objectives for each category with a 3 to 5 year outlook. Be specific with each goal. Think of how the goal(s) will be measured and describe. Describe if they are a challenge, yet attainable. Give thought if the goal is relevant to your life and you outlook on achievements. Ensure that all goals are time bound. If you need to list notes to flesh out with a mentor, please list.

1. Family: When I asked Ann for her 3 to 5 year goal for her family she quickly went to her son. Obviously being a parent helps define your focus. Ann spoke that her goal for her son is to have grades good enough for college and a passion he has defined for a direction for his life. This is a good goal, but I pushed her for more definition. What type of grades? She replied 3.2 or higher. Then I asked what type of passion. She stated that her desire, and his at the present, was for a degree in chemical engineering, to work in this field or to teach, as he likes helping others. But he would also consider a business degree. So we listed that out as a family goal.

2. Financial: Ann responded that she would like to be financially independent and to own a home. At present she and her husband have always rented. I pushed deeper on the financial independence and she stated that they have always lived paycheck to paycheck. So I suggested we write a goal with specifics and timelines using the

SMART Goal method.[2] We defined the goal specifics as: To own a home in 3-years with the ability to save 15% of income for savings.

3. Physical: Here Ann spoke that she would like both her and her husband to become active together, as well as to get into shape. I asked what would be the goal on any weight loss? What would be the goal on activity? She defined the goal as each losing about 20-pounds and maintaining it, she would like to see that obtained within six months. On activity she stated her goal would be for each of them to commit to visit a local gym three times a week, morning or evenings. She would like to see that started and executed consistently within two months, so they can arrange schedules.

4. Mental: Everyone needs to understand that mental fitness is important. Exercising your mental muscle and challenging it will help one with stress and patience. Ann thought about this one a while. She believes that if she can read one book a month, whether for work or for enjoyment, but just read and enjoy, that it would help her mentally. She stated that reading relaxes her and allows her to meditate. This goal was pretty precise, although one can define what types of books to read if they feel the need.

5. Spiritual: On this topic I always coach that I will not judge, as many have different interpretations of spiritual. But with Ann, hers were more grounded in the Christian faith in which she was raised. She spoke about believing in

2 George T. Doran, *There Is A S.M.A.R.T. Way To Write Management Goals And Objectives*

the faith, but perhaps straying or not being consistent. Her goal was to become part of a bible study that meets at least twice a month. She knows her church has those available and wants to become active within one.

6. Career: Number six is career. She and I will expand on this more within additional exercises. But here is a good opportunity to define an early goal that will help us with her vision. She stated that within three years that she would like to be a group manager, which in our business is just above a team lead. So this means she would have to be promoted twice within two years. Which is achievable, but a little aggressive.

This was a good exercise that provided solid insight. Now I wanted Ann to think of a few things in a different direction. I asked her a question that I was asked many years ago, that really allowed me to think about how I would want to be remembered. So the question is, what would you want people to say about you at your funeral? This may not be as specific as a goal, with a timeline and measures. But it does truly make you think about how you want to live your life so that everyone at your funeral would have the same perception. Neighbors, fellow workers, family and friends, what would you want them to say? This may actually point back to your foundation of values and principles, as the answer should have alignment. I once listed mine as everyone stating, "He was a good man." Simple, yes, but my belief is that if everyone made this statement about me, then I at least lived my values, and contributed to others, and was respected for who I was. Ann wrote down three different items and then read her choice. "She was passionate that everyone lived their lives to the fullest." Ann believed that if this was said it certainly would define how she lived with passion and focus. We tested it, by asking a few random individuals. "What would you think if everyone at a funeral has this one thing to say about the person that passed?" When we asked, the responses were in alignment with what Ann had stated. This told us that the statement was a solid one to utilize.

I had a couple more questions to round out the exercise. I asked Ann, if she had all the means in the world and did not have to work, what would she spend her days and time on. Her response was quick. She stated that she would donate time and effort in helping women who were abused. This was an awesome answer, but it made me ask her why it was not part of her goals? She became silent and then admitted she probably has always believed it was so hard to achieve, and therefore not set it as a goal but only as a dream. This is where the exercise paid dividends in bringing this insight out. A dream will only be a dream without a goal and a plan. So I coached her to take the next step and make it a goal. In time, we can make it a reality. The other purpose of the exercise is to help a person understand, that goals are meant to be shared. As it is often others, that when they believe in your goal with you, sometimes are a part of you achieving it. This is why my mother would always tell me to find mentors and then pay it forward. She believed it was important to mentor others and keep the cycle going.

So the next step was to develop and define a personal Vision Statement. I wanted Ann to push herself with a vision that she would have to reach for, stretch herself and her development, as well as exhaust herself to obtain. Remember, a Vision Statement needs to be 3 to 5 years looking ahead, with a Big Hairy Audacious Goal. Here is where one may need not be humble, but allow their ego to believe that they can achieve. In addition, some BHAG's may state something we as individuals may not view as big and hairy, or audacious.

• • • • • • • • • • •

Remember, a Vision Statement needs to be 3 to 5 years looking ahead, with a Big Hairy Audacious Goal.

• • • • • • • • • • •

This is because we each perceive ourselves and our capabilities differently. In some ways we each have to face that voice in our head that tries to hold us back. I call this facing your giant. Here is where it sometimes becomes very personal. I asked Ann to take a day and really think about what is a giant that she has had in her life that she knows she needs to face, but has always been hesitant to? This can be a person, a perception or a belief brought on by either or both.

Ann and I met the next day to further the discussion. Ann was a little reserved at the start of the meeting. When we started to discuss the Vision Statement, I asked Ann what was the giant that she would need to face. We do this exercise because many times it is that giant that will be the cause or hindrance to success. Facing ones giant is also life changing as it teaches confrontation as a benefit and perseverance, which is important to all leaders. When Ann started to speak, her voice quivered a little. This quickly made me aware that Ann definitely dug down deep to identify her giant, and it was very personal. Fortunately, I had also earned enough trust with Ann for her to proceed with the exercise as her hunger to develop and grow was stronger than the urge to keep it within herself. This is a barrier that must be surpassed or it will continue to be a roadblock. One must genuinely determine if they truly will face their giant and overcome the issue. Ann was ready.

I asked Ann to explain and define her giant. She stated that she had a personal perception that she was not good enough to accomplish developing into a leader. This is not uncommon, but we must address where the perception comes from. As we spoke it was apparent that Ann believed this is what she hears from her spouse, and this is why it is so personal and truly a giant. She loved her spouse and believed it was important to raise her son with his father, but she had allowed herself to be controlled by his belief system. As we continued deeper, she admitted she had allowed him, over time, to talk her out of some of her dreams and goals. Not that he was forcefully dominant, but he was not too supportive and verbally would express his lack of support or belief in her. As this became common she had allowed herself to lack drive to take action on many of her goals. She stated that this was why when she applied for her current role that being an Administrative Assistant was the only aspiration she had. It was when she saw she could grow and others recognized her for her abilities that she started to imagine herself growing again.

Here is a delicate balance in managing that is important. To become a great leader one must learn to face their giants. Many times those giants are at home. Our role in building leaders is to be supportive, while at times being a sounding block, and possibly suggesting resources. Ultimately it is the individual who must decide if they are going to face their giant and move forward. Ann needed to decide that if she was going to proceed in her development that she would work on the situation with her giant, with a commitment to still move forward. Many times a person who is a naysayer is simply silenced when they see that their negative words are having no effect. At times, it is the naysayer that has something to overcome, like a complex of being in control. At other times there are some that do not realize how they may come across. In marriages, I believe it is important to communicate the situation and commit to improving the situation for a better marriage. Ann decided that she needed to address the situation with her spouse. She was pleased that he was open to the conversation and apologized if he had come across that way to her. He stated that he would be proud and supportive of Ann developing farther. He did admit that he may have felt that if she improved herself that she may find someone else. Ann assured him of her love and commitment and they both agreed to be more open about any insecurities. Facing her giant with this conversation paid huge dividends. But sometimes it may have to be addressed again.

So now it was time for Ann to define her Vision Statement. With her giant being addressed, and now if she believed she would have support or no support, would she push herself to overcome it? What could she accomplish? What is truly her outlook? If she lived her dream, what would that be?

Ann stated that in 3 to 5 years she wanted to be financially independent. I responded by asking her to define that in detail. Financially independent to one person may be different to another. I pushed her to put details around what financially independent means to her. She thought about it for a moment and she stated, "I believe if I made a consistent income of $65,000 or better, that would bring me to financial independence."

I then asked, "Describe how that brings you to financial independence?"

Ann replied, "One, it pays my bills with good allotment for saving, as well as additional expenses I may incur. It would be twice of what I make now."

"That is a good answer to start. Let's break it down some more," I replied.

Ann thought some more. "When I have thought about this, I picked this number because I believe it allows me to be independent even if I was not married. This figure is not reliant on any other income. Now I pray and plan to stay married, but being able to be at a place where financially I could be independent is a comfortable place to be. Next, when I looked at the figures I believe I would be able to save 10% to 15% of my income for savings. After all, I would like the ability to buy a home, instead of always renting."

Ann was now working the exercise well. What also impressed me was how very evident it was that she has already been giving this thought. Which is a solid sign of an aspiring leader. I asked Ann, "So tell me about the house you would like to buy?"

Ann was quick to answer, "Well, I have been looking at these three bedroom homes that this certain builder builds. They build them across this city, but I would like to move to the northwest area where the traffic is less and the schools have a good reputation. Good schools for my son are important. Traveling in to the office is a little sacrifice for what I want."

"That is awesome, so you have been dreaming about this already?" I pressed.

"Yes," she said with a big smile. "I have had my husband drive with me on the weekends and we have visited the model homes. He likes them as well. So you could say we both have the dream. But I also believe it is smart to base any large investment like a house, on one income. One time my husband was injured and off work, so that incident was a valuable lesson. If we are both working then we save more, or put more into the house."

"That is wise advice," I complimented. "So let's write down when your goal would be to buy the house, based upon what you can save, and how you can advance on your job role and income."

Ann wrote on her notepad. To be financially independent, that is 3-years to be able to purchase a new 3-bedroom home in the northwest side of the city. I had her also write down to be earning an annual salary equal to or greater than $65,000.

"Now let's think about your professional position, title and role that you would like to obtain and the time frame," I added.

Ann spoke up, "I believe I already stated that in my goals, that I would like to have earned the promotion of a Group Manager, which also matches the income scenario."

"I can see you have given that some thought already," I replied with a small grin.

"Yes, I think about it all the time," she answered, eagerly.

"Great," I said. "So the last tie in is what you can be doing to help others?"

"Well, I already mentioned about helping abused women," she stated.

"Yes, you did. So let's get a little more specific. How much can you do 3-years from now? How much of your time and efforts would you want to push yourself to?" I asked.

Ann gave it some thought. "I believe that if I can be in a position to be an active member of a group, giving at least one day a week, and then grow it from there."

"That sounds reasonable. Now with your expected growth in knowledge and advancement in leadership how would you want to utilize that to mentor others?" I asked.

"That is a good question," she responded. "First, I would want to still have mentors, but I would like to have at least a couple of individuals I mentor."

"That could also be someone from your work with abused women," I stated.

She smiled, "That would be awesome, as that can be their way of perhaps getting themselves out of the situation."

"Absolutely," I agreed. "I can see that tie in together. I believe we have enough to draft your vision statement. Are you ready to give it an attempt?"

Ann gave a grimacing look, it was actually a little funny. But I am sure it was just a nervous feeling of taking that next step and drafting a Vision Statement that will be hers. She would own it, push towards it, and with perseverance, she would live it. I informed Ann that I would let her work on it for 30-minutes and then we would sync up again. I told her to perhaps draft several and test how they flow and sound. Ann acknowledged the task and started on the process.

I went and worked on other work items that were on my to do list. I was pleased with the session with Ann. While working with an aspiring leader, the sessions also allowed me to gain insight based upon the interaction. One item that showed this was a positive factor, was that it was evident that Ann had already been thinking of her goals and aspirations. She already knew and assessed her dreams and was driven to obtain her objectives. There are intangibles that are inherent in future leaders. Leaders have a hunger for growth, to help others and to not settle for mediocrity. Ann demonstrated that hunger through our session. Also, when working through the process and evaluation, it was evident that others already perceived Ann as a leader and her potential for growth. To be a leader it is not necessary that you are a manager, as a leader is a person that gains followers and rallies the troops. It was evident that Ann rallies the troops and serves those she can.

After 30-minutes working on other things, I met Ann in the conference room where she and I were working earlier. Ann was writing on the whiteboard and had three scenarios of a Vision Statement lined out. This is the nice part of having the conference room available; by having a whiteboard accessible to work on ideas. If not, notepads are a second alternative and effective. I walked in and Ann turned and smiled, then stepped back to look at her choices.

Ann then circled one, letting me know this was her choice. I read through it. "Within 3-years, to obtain financial independence earning an annual income of $65,000 or greater, and purchasing a 3-bedroom home while having the ability to save 10% or more from income. To earn two promotions obtaining the role of Group Manager with my current employer, and utilize my skills, expertise and blessings to donate one day per week working with abused women. Finally, paying it forward by mentoring two women at a time, that aspire to become leaders and advance."

Ann did a good job. A Vision Statement can be a bit wordy, as it is internal facing, so it faces you. Because it expands in several areas this allows for its wordiness. A Mission Statement should be concise and direct, as that is external facing. A Mission Statement is your purpose and a Vision Statement is what you are driving to. Your Values and Principles are the foundation and every decision, strategy and direction are driven from there. If they do not match the foundation, then you are straying from your foundation and that is when problems arise.

Ann was excited and wanted to create a flyer that encompasses her Principle Statements she created along with her Mission Statement, and now also her Vision Statement. She wanted this to hang at home, as

A Mission Statement is your purpose and a Vision Statement is what you are driving to.

well as at work. Not only as a reminder for her, but also as an accountability to others that view it. If she states these are my principles and showcases them, then it is important that she demonstrates them. By demonstrating her Mission and her Vision Statements she is also letting others know what she is asking them to hold her accountable on. This is a great exercise and highly recommended. Ann created and displayed her flyer prominently.

Ann's Principle Statements

Respect yourself first and demonstrate respect for others.

Earn trust daily and reward others that do the same.

Seek fun in all you do and let others enjoy and celebrate success.

Passion is the objective, results are the achievement.

Execute with initiative and seek innovation.

Count accountability as your responsibility to yourself and others.

Taste the hunger for what feeds you and drives you to the next level.

Ann's Mission Statement:

To seek solutions and betterment of myself and others through compassion and effort, and to face the future with an optimistic outlook.

Ann's Vision Statement:

Within 3-years, to obtain financial independence earning an annual income of $65,000 or greater, and purchasing a 3-bedroom home while having the ability to save 10% or more from income. To earn two promotions obtaining the role of Group Manager with my current employer, and utilize my skills, expertise and blessings to donate one day per week working with abused women. Finally, paying it forward by mentoring two women at a time, that aspire to become leaders and advance.

End

Define your personal development goals:

With the creation of Ann's Mission, Vision and Values that include her principles much has been discussed about Ann's goals. This is part of the process to help define the basis of her goals. The exercise in Chapter 1 allowed Ann to assess her gifts and abilities. These traits were for leadership and gave Ann great insight into current status as well as future development. Now Ann needs to define and spell out her personal development goals. These are goals that increase personal development that benefit Ann no matter where she may work, while they also benefit her professionally.

I asked Ann to do an exercise and bring it back to our scheduled meeting the next day. I tasked and challenged her to break down some of her goals in three categories. When you think about personal development goals, the challenge is to define what are short-term, then what are long-term and finally, what are legacy goals. Short-term goals are the ones to be achieved within a year, two years maximum. Certain short-term goals should be designed as stepping stones for accomplishing long-term goals. Perhaps a skill, knowledge, home, or accomplishment that opens the door and opportunity for that long-term dream. Long-term goals are ones that will take longer than that time frame. These will take into account lifestyle, family and career. This would be a mindset of where you would want to be 5 to 20-years from now. Finally, legacy goals define the legacy you want to leave behind. What do you want to leave as a legacy to society and family? What do you want to be known as?

My brother has long-term goals of retirement at age 60. Unfortunately, too many individuals do not think of retirement early enough. Human nature tells us we have plenty of time to think of this. I look at my son and I am impressed how much farther along he is with this concept than I was at his age. This is an important concept to teach and work with those you mentor to consider. Most of the time, short-term goals are more pressing as they usually deal with current finances and debt. But if they are not addressed and placed in a plan, the cycle seldom gets corrected. My legacy goals deal with being remembered as inspiring a new generation of leaders. I work well with millennials and believe they are the most courageous workforce there is. A huge part of my legacy is the development of aspiring women for leadership development. A legacy goal for my family is to be remembered as a man of good character, as well as to have provided a foundation for future education and development opportunities for generations of my offspring. So these are some examples I explained and provided on a worksheet for Ann and she acknowledged her understanding of the task. We agreed to meet the next day.

Mark Villareal
People, Strategy, Execution

Personal Development Goals

Break down your Personal Development Goals. Think of your goals and separate in three categories.

Short-term Goals: To be achieved in 1 to 2 years maximum. This can be a stepping stone or a building block to larger goals and achievements. This can be development of skills, knowledge gain or an achievement that is a foundation for greater success.

Long-Term Goals: These goals take longer with a 5 to 20 year outlook. Think about lifestyle, family, and long-term professional aspirations. This can also be goals that make an impact of others.

Legacy Goals: What legacy do you want to leave behind (Society, family)? What do you want to be known as or remembered for?

The next day, Ann was ready to meet. She did ask at the start if there was a certain order that she should have defined her goals. I explained that I did not direct her to execute in a certain order, so I could see her thought process. Ann stated that she gave it some thought as she initially believed that creating her long-term goals first might help her then break down her short-term goals. But after she started the process, she struggled with the idea that it might be easier to build and attack the short-term goals first, as those would be the foundation for her long-term goals. I appreciated her thought process. Both ways work and I have seen individuals do it either way. However, there is training and a book that I had not yet assigned to Ann titled *Seven Habits of Highly Effective People.* One of the habits is to start with the end in mind. Which means to define what you believe the end should look like and then build what it takes to get there. This works great as a habit. So I recommend creating it in this way.

Ann and I met in the conference room. I suggested that she utilize the whiteboard in the room and present to me what she came up with. She grabbed her notepad, walked over to the board and started listing her long-term goals. As she started numbering them, she started speaking.

1. To own a home with no mortgage within 20-years. This is a good goal, as she does not own a current home, so this is pushing herself to get in a position to purchase a home and either pay it off with a 15-year loan or pay it off early.

I asked her what her thoughts were on how she would pay it off?

"From what I have studied, you can get a 30-year loan, and if you can make one extra payment a year, in other words, make 13 payments instead of 12, then the extra payment saves on accumulating interest and it shaves 8-years off that loan. This means the home is paid for in 22-years, which I would then look at paying extra deeper into the loan or just pay the balance off at 20-years," she explained.

I was pleased that Ann had a sharp and educated answer. She had a plan that was accurate and well thought out. On long-term goals the intent is to show within the exercise what will get you close enough to achieve the goal. This is what you would call getting within striking distance. Ann continued and wrote number two on the board.

2. To have invested into two rental properties, that are revenue-generating, that covers the mortgage, as well as a safe balance that helps with upkeep and repairs. I asked her to tell me any thoughts she had with the details of the plan.

Ann replied, "My husband and I can manage them, but a property manager is 10% on average should we decide to have them managed. From what I have learned from others who do have properties, is that a property manager does provide a buffer between a renter and the owner. Also, a property manager does background checks and is held accountable for timely payments, so they hold the renters accountable."

"Very good," I replied. I appreciated her efforts so far.

3. 401K of $200,000 or more, from my salary, not including husbands. (20-years)

Ann started explaining before I could ask anything. "I defined what I have committed to saving from each paycheck and I have challenged my husband to do the same, but here I am relying on my commitment. This averages $10,000 per year, which means I would need to make more money. But I also found on the internet this chart that I plugged into that shows average investment growth is 8%, but I factored at 7%, to be a little conservative. Then I ramped up my investing as the years developed." Ann showed me a printed chart.

"Ann, I think you did a great job with your long-term goals," I complimented her.

Ann smiled. "Thanks," she replied.

"Now I know you may have more long-term goals, and each year you need to evaluate them," I continued. "Besides, you will develop a few more as time goes by. Good job on what you have done so far."

• • • • • • • • • • •

To have continuous improvement and advancement, commit to knowledge and development in both personal and professional skills.

• • • • • • • • • • •

Note that these long-term goals were personal, but it would have to take the execution of solid professional goals to achieve these. To have success with professional goals there are knowledge and skills development that are both personal and professional that have to be recognized and committed to for one to have continuous improvement and advancement. The assessments we had Ann and her peers do may provide some insight, but this is where good mentorship provides guidance in building a plan.

Ann asked if I wanted her to start writing her short-term personal goals on the board, as she had a list ready. I asked her how many did she come up with. She said she narrowed them down to 10, as some she decided were somewhat duplicates, or similar enough to combine. When I mentor others, I usually try for us to define a minimum of 10 or more.

"Before you start, let me ask some questions that may enlighten you, as you may not have thought of some things that would give insight into your list creation," I proposed.

"Okay," Ann responded. She looked in my direction, ready to hear the questions.

"Okay, first, based upon your long-term goals, what knowledge or skills do you lack or that you know you need to develop further for those to be accomplished?" I asked.

Ann looked at the whiteboard and reread the list to herself. You could hear her read, though not clear enough to know what she read, but it was obvious she was thinking about the question while reviewing each long-term goal.

"I do know I need to learn more about finances, financial planning, and taxes," Ann responded. "So I would want to take a course on that. Our church offers some courses on personal financial management. But I would also like to understand small business financial management, which I know the Community College offers."

"Excellent, so that should be a short-term goal," I stated. "So let's write that down. We will list out the particulars before we are done."

"Okay," she said with a smile. She seemed a little excited, as though she saw herself perhaps accomplishing something.

"Next question," I continued. "It is obvious you need to earn more money. I know you want to advance. But what is that going to take in development that will assist you personally and professionally?"

Ann stood silent for a little while, evidently stumped.

"What traits do strong leaders have, as well as strong contributors in society?" I asked.

"They have strong emotional intelligence," Ann replied.

"Great, you are correct!" I exclaimed. "Anything else. What next?"

"They are strong communicators and influencers," Ann continued.

"Correct, so let's write those three things down and talk about if these are skills you need to develop further. Also, how would these benefit you personally, or would they?" I asked.

Ann was quick to respond. "I believe each item would benefit me. Being a good communicator would help me when discussing options on investment homes, finances and everything else that is involved. Being a good influencer is essential in dealing with potential tenants and property managers. Learning better skills in emotional intelligence is essential in dealing with different people in different ways."

"I would agree. So you can see how much of your personal goals do drive your professional goals as well, especially in developmental areas." I turned my laptop so Ann could see what I had on my screen. I had executed a search on courses within the development of empathy, which is the key aspect of emotional intelligence. I showed Ann that there was a course at the local Community College. This would have solid value as she would interact with others. There were online courses available too. She seemed excited.

"This looks great. I know I can arrange a night course or two," she stated, confidently.

"The big thing is to first identify what, then to prioritize when," I explained. "Write down empathy development, communication development, as well as persuasion and influencing others. So now you have three more items on your personal goals. We will flesh out the details when we have the whole list."

She looked thoughtful as she replied, "I need to look at my list that I made last night and see if there is any that correlate to what I just added, or if they are all different."

"Good idea," I agreed. Ann sat down and reviewed her list while making some notes.

"Okay, so what other questions should I consider?" Ann asked.

"I think it is the same question. What are some traits that strong leaders must have or traits you already know about yourself that you would need and want to improve that would benefit you personally as well?" I inquired.

"Well, one of the things you state all of the time is that confrontation is a benefit, which means I need to not be afraid to confront and address issues. I know if I eventually have a rental property that I would have to confront issues and hold tenants accountable. In buying and maintaining a home I would have to be able to speak up about any concerns or I would only have myself to blame," Ann contemplated.

"Can you see that by doing long-term goals and then asking these questions that you can drive home the list and needs of short-term development goals?" I asked her.

Ann nodded her head. "Yes, and to accomplish this I need better habits and a routine. That would probably give me time back at home, as well as make me more effective at work."

"Bingo!" I exclaimed. "This is coming together well. Write down 'forming better habits', and also 'becoming more assertive', as that is where the confrontation comes in. Being a better communicator and influencer are additional traits for that confrontation. They bring balance."

Ann took a moment to write her list on the board.

1. Financial Management
2. Empathy Development (Emotional Intelligence)
3. Communication Development
4. Persuasion / Influence
5. Assertiveness
6. Habits

"This is a pretty good list, very specific," Ann affirmed.

"Yes, it is. This one, with the others, will have its challenges. Does that create any additional needs?" I asked.

"Yes, I will have to be organized and disciplined, as well as have more determination. Is there a way I can build more determination?" she questioned.

"I believe so," I answered. "Many times there are several factors that can influence that. You already have better habits. There is also overcoming adversity, as well as being more strategically focused."

"Wow, I see where I could use both of those. Certainly in my personal life there will be challenges, especially if we obtain rental properties. I am sure strategy is important when you list places for rent, where you list and how you maximize value," Ann remarked.

"I like how you think about it personally first and you see how it helps you there. Then professionally," I commented. "So which ones sound correct to you?"

"Both," she decided. She added overcoming adversity and strategic thinking to her list.

"Okay, Ann. You have a list of 8, which is a solid list. You can probably write resilience next to overcoming adversity. Think hard about what would be your next ones. We can always come up with more, but if we choose 10 to focus and develop a plan around, as well as execute, your development will jump leaps and bounds," I explained.

Ann stood silent for a moment. This is the point sometimes where a suggestion would help.

"Ann, for you to buy property, invest or other personal things that will arise, do you have a formal thought process on making decisions?" I asked.

"Not really," she answered. She sounded as though she was embarrassed.

"Don't let it bother you if you do not yet. When you are first starting out, life is not that complicated. However, this is why so many people live paycheck to paycheck because it is also part of life being easy. Some fall into blessings that teach them, others fall into struggles where they either have to learn or fail. Failure is a big teacher," I explained.

"You have said that right!" Ann responded. "There was a time when our water heater went out unexpectedly and we had to go for two weeks with no hot water. Even then, we had to borrow the money. That is when I told myself, I must take steps to grow."

"Nothing motivates you more than a cold shower," I said, while laughing. "But let's add decision-making to your list."

Ann wrote decision-making on her list. Then she spoke, "What about better listening skills?"

"That is always a good one," I concurred. "Great leaders listen well. In fact, what makes this skill effective is not just hearing what someone says, but having the ability to understand and demonstrate to that person that you comprehend. Summarizing what you heard is what makes an impact on good listening skills. I had a great mentor that used to say that sometimes it is what is not said, and also someone's body language as well. If you believe that one belongs on your list, then let's write it down.

Ann thought about it for a moment then nodded her head in agreement. She added it to her list.

1. Financial Management
2. Empathy Development (Emotional Intelligence)
3. Communication Development
4. Persuasion / Influence
5. Assertiveness
6. Habits
7. Overcoming Adversity / Resilience
8. Strategic Thinking
9. Decision-making
10. Listening skills

Ann had a great list. These are 10 solid personal goals that will also cross over and benefit Ann in her professional goals. But this is also where walking the person through the exercise is important, as this becomes a realization to them through the process. To complete them, an Action Plan will be required to be built around them to ensure and hold accountable for the execution. SMART Goals will be invaluable as they flesh everything out with specifics. Before that, I worked with Ann on her professional goals, which may be the same as they do parallel. But there are usually a few goals added to that. Ann and I had accomplished much on this day. So we scheduled for the same time in the morning and I tasked her with re-evaluating the list we created for personal goals.

I also asked her to define that which, if all or only some, cross over to her professional goals. Then, what traits or skills other than the ones listed would be added for her professional advancement. This truly shows that personal development goals are a foundation of professional development goals. Ann wrote a few notes before returning to her normal work area.

Create Professional Development Goals:

Ann and I met the next day at the same time in the conference room. She came in and stated upfront that defining more skills or traits for development for her professional goals only, which would add to her personal goals, was a challenge. This is not uncommon and it generally deals with understanding the mindset that it takes to be a leader. Leadership traits are valuable in everyday interaction. But leadership traits outside of everyday interaction with the mindset of traits for a profession is a little different. Think of it this way. If you are leading a business, and need to lead people, what traits would you encounter on your way to success? What challenges will arise and what skills will be needed to overcome those challenges and still arrive at a high level? Everything she placed in her personal development goals crossed over to her professional development goals too. But what is missing or can be added?

This is where mentoring takes place. Depending on how long the person has been around helps decide their understanding of what they have witnessed. If that person has seen changes, and through that change then witnessed the transformation and success of the business, then they have seen and witnessed change management. If they have not witnessed this and started when things were okay, then mentoring them through examples of other times or other businesses is an exercise to walk through. I teach that great companies have to reinvent themselves and be innovative to survive. This is especially true of Apple, Microsoft and other technology companies. They constantly innovate and create, or they falter. When you walk through tangible examples, then those being mentored can identify. Then with those examples you can still point to hurdles and roadblocks that the organization had to encounter. Through this exercise you can then identify a few more items.

Change Management: Obviously to reinvent yourself, you have to be led by a leader who has strong change management skills. These skills are the ability to lead a team through change that, with a process, increases accountability, ownership, trust, tenacity and focus. Individuals need to believe the vision. To be a leader one has to have followers. To get others to follow is a skill, not a command. So I walked Ann through our history and how the organization was once several hundred thousand dollars in debt with daily problems. She was surprised. I walked her through how

> *To be a leader one has to have followers. To get others to follow is a skill, not a command.*

we had to rebuild culture and attack it immediately. We built strategy and shared the vision to gain ownership and accountability. I spoke of our struggles, challenges and the roadblocks that occurred. I explained how we pushed with tenacity and raised expectations to climb the mountain to success. I asked Ann, with these stories and examples, what traits or skills would a leader need?

"Change Management skills, obviously," Ann declared.

"What else?" I asked.

Ann thought for a moment. "A leader would need to get people to follow and believe," she continued.

"True, so how does one do that?" I pushed.

"By earning trust," she replied. "But is that a skill?"

"Yes, it is," I answered. "It is one of the most needed skills. Why would this skill be needed?" I asked Ann.

"Because at first, they may respond because of the person's title or position, but after a while, it all moves to trust. If they trust that leader more, they will believe and execute," Ann explained.

Ann had her thought process dead on. A leader must earn trust, not demand trust. A title or position may give someone authority, but trust gives that person command. Individuals have a natural sense to follow a leader who earns their trust. So I had Ann write Earn Trust on the whiteboard along with Change Management. Then I sat silent and looked at her for the next answer.

"What?" she said, with a smile.

"What else?" I asked. "What other things arise through a person leading a team, or organization, especially when earning trust and conducting change management?"

"I suppose there would be conflict. Conflict with management, departments with departments, or person with person," she said, thoughtfully.

Ann was proving to be pretty sharp with her answers, which was exciting. "Yes, of course, this just happens. A strong leader will recognize it, address it and overcome the conflict. Not all conflict is bad, sometimes it is just a difference in opinion. But not managing conflict is bad and it will create more," I elaborated.

Ann added conflict resolution to her list on the whiteboard. She turned to indicate like she was done, but I sat in silence again.

"What?" she asked, incredulously.

"Is there anything else?" I pressed.

This is where she appeared to be stumped. This is not unnatural at this stage.

"Humility," I declared. "The best leaders need to work daily on their trait and skill of humility. Remember, humility is a strength, not a weakness. The best leaders apologize, admit when they are wrong, appreciate others and understand they learn from others no matter their title or position."

Ann agreed and stated that is what she likes most about our organization. Her immediate supervisor, as well as other supervisors, have a good grasp of leading with humility. She expressed that she witnessed that this starts at the top and she appreciated it. She saw that employees are free to share opinions and even disagreements, but they do so respectfully. She knows this is the culture that has been developed and because others can share ideas, the organization is better for it. Ann's professional goals consisted of her 10-personal goals with 4 professional goals added on.

1. Change Management
2. Conflict Resolution
3. Trust
4. Humility

We listed these on a worksheet with brief definitions to assist in our next step and to maintain in her file. Our next step was now to build an Action Plan around these goals.

Mark Villareal
People, Strategy, Execution

Personal Development Goals

Break down your long-term goals, both personal and professional to determine what short-term development goals in skills and knowledge that is needed for their achievement. Keep a mind-set that these goals are a 1 to 2 year outlook for completion. It is highly recommended to work with a mentor who has achieved success personally and professionally.

List Personal Short-Term Development Goals (up to 10):

1. Financial Management – Understanding personal finance and investment.
2. Empathy (Emotional Intelligence) – developing and managing the understanding of individuals different make-ups.
3. Communication – Developing the skills of effective communication, tied with the knowledge of Emotional Intelligence.
4. Persuasion / Influence – To learn the skills and knowledge to persuade and influence others as a leader that gains commitment and followers.
5. Assertiveness – To learn that confrontation is a benefit and how to be assertive effectively that others maintain mutual respect.
6. Habits – To define, learn, and consistently put forth good habits that drive good results and accountability.

7. Overcoming Adversity / Resilience – To gain the ability to face, overcome, and flourish through adversity. To demonstrate resilience when working through obstacles and setbacks.

8. Decision-Making – To define a proper method of decision-making that brings the right solutions. To be consistent and decisive with confidence.

9. Listening Skills – To be an effective listener, showing proper focus and attention that earns respect and demonstrates the importance of gaining understanding.

List Professional Short-Term Development Goals (Approximately 4)

1. Change Management – To develop the leadership skills that demonstrate effective change management that leads a team through proper change achieving the objective and outcome.

2. Conflict Resolution – To understand and comprehend proper conflict resolution, and develop the skills to implement with teams and individuals.

3. Trust – To learn the importance and different aspects of trust that earns trust daily, and teaches others to do the same.

4. Humility – To always lead with humility to be a servant leader and while learning from others and understanding different viewpoints.

End

Action Plan Development:

There are many different levels of Action Plans for development. The key points are listing each item and breaking it down to the different tasks, pieces of training, tests and evaluations that must be done. Defining when, as well as who needs to be involved, and what needs to be involved is important. The plan answers who, what, when, where, why and how. Each must be specific, which is the first letter of a SMART Goal. This is then followed by how each will be measured. The next letter is if the goal is attainable? Attainable can be within the time frame or by the accomplishment itself. If the item is reliant on others, how does that affect its attainability? By answering and defining this we then test if it is relevant. Does it make sense for the role? Does it create an improvement? The final element is if it is time-bound, as it must have a time commitment.

I walked Ann through a printed template that I like to use. I let her know that I will email her the template in a spreadsheet so she can insert her comments and each corresponding piece of information. I demonstrated that one item can have several components that tie to the goal, so each sub-component would be listed on a separate line under the main goal. The importance is thinking through the whole process in detail with each task required for accomplishing the goal. The better the detail the better the execution and results.

* * * * * * * * * * *

The better the detail the better the execution and results.

* * * * * * * * * * *

The spreadsheet has a place for the employee's name, position, date and manager's name. The first item within the plan to be filled in is Action Plan Specifics. This is where you would first list the goal. I instructed Ann to list 1. Financial Management. Then, I told her that anything we come up with related to Financial Management would go in the rows underneath. I explained that we simply use the tab key for one tab space underneath Financial Management which demonstrates underneath the goal that it is a sub-component of the goal. I knew that as we fleshed this out more she would have a better understanding as the visible spread-sheet was being completed.

The next column list was for the owner's name. Although these goals were Ann's, others may own responsibility or share responsibility and will be relied upon to assist in the execution. It is important to list anyone who plays a role in assisting in accomplishing the goal when building the plan. This is because if for any reason they cannot play that role, you need to be aware of that at the start and not when it may be critical. Any name on the list has to agree to be on the list and to own or share that responsibility. They must be aware of all aspects, timelines, and the definition of completion as well as execution. The next column is titled Measure. This is asking what the measure will be. This can be 100% completion, a pass rate of 80% if it is an exam or certification, or a result of achievement. It is important to list the specifics.

Ann appeared to be comprehending, but I also knew that as we developed the plan, she would have moments of clearer understanding. The next column is the Due Date column. This is when the task or what is on the Action Item for that row is to be completed. The final column is for comments for the row. These comments can be before, during or after for that Action item. At the bottom of the Action Plan is a color code legend stating that red signifies that the item is not started. Yellow signifies that the item is in progress, while green defines that it is completed. This is for a visual and a quick snapshot of the plan in action at any given point. I explained to Ann, as I would with any employee, that we would place this on a shared drive so we can both witness the progress at any moment. With others that I have mentored, that did not work in the same organization as myself, we utilized shared available drive services. I recommended that Ann keep it updated as actions occur, as well as to review it once a week on a set day as a routine. We agreed that each Monday she would have the plan updated and this would allow me to view after each Monday with the reassurance of its accuracy.

With Ann's first goal being Financial Management this was listed in the first row. Ann was the owner and the measurement would be two certificates of completion. We explained the two courses within the comments section and made the due dates for 18-months from the current date due to the timing of courses. It would also allow for other action items within this goal. The next rows were the individual breakdowns. The Community College course was listed with each detail explained as was the Dave Ramsey course. However, I then showed Ann some online courses that the organization had available, at a small cost, and showed her the objectives for each course. Believing Ann would accomplish the first two listed I explained that we, as an organization, would then invest and pay for these for her education and advancement. Ann was touched and excited by this, but these are the exact motivators employers should provide. An educated developing and motivated employee is a good employee to have. I defined with Ann that an 80% pass rate would be required for us to pay for the course.

The course allows you to retest, but understanding the content will take a commitment. We as employers need to build a commitment through accountability from those we invest in. Ann committed, so we listed these items. We then walked through the next goal.

Ann wrote down the next goal and we worked the same way. The whole goal itself, we gave 18-months to complete. Then we also listed the Community College course we discovered. Ann committed that she could take these two courses at night for the same semester. We did discuss, however, that two at the same time would be the maximum commitment, no more. It is important to set goals that may be a challenge but to not over commit.

• • • • • • • • • • • •

It is important to set goals that may be a challenge but to not over commit.

• • • • • • • • • • •

Individuals always believe, due to excitement, that they can accomplish a lot. It is good to have that excitement, but they tend to want to over commit. We as leaders must help them build their programs for success. When individuals over commit, at some point they see the failure and feel the stress. I at times would even build their programs where they became more difficult gradually, as time went by, so they could witness success and be well vested in its completion. Ann and I worked more on her plan, and it took two days of meetings to line out. When completed I had asked Ann, is this what you will live for? She answered with an emphatic yes. Here a snapshot of a point in time of a few of her goals within her Development Action Plan.

Development Action Plan

Employee Name:				Date:
Ann Bolings				**06/04/2019**
Job Role:				**Manager:**
Admin Assistant				**Gary Hitton**

Action Item: Specifics	Owner:	Measure:	Due Date:	Comments
1. Financial Management	**Ann**	**Two Certs**	**1/1/2021**	**One Cert CC & Other Ramsey Course**
Community College semester program	Ann	Cert / 80%	2/1/2020	Certificate of completion at 80% grade
Dave Ramsey – Financial Management	Ann	Completion	3/1/2021	Dave Ramsey – through church
Accounting for non-professionals	Mark / Ann	80%	6/1/2021	Online course – Company to pay
Budgeting for business	Mark / Ann	80%	10/1/2021	Online course – Company to pay
2. Empathy Development / EQ	**Ann**	**Cert**	**1/1/2020**	**Increasing understanding of EQ**
Understanding Empathy & EQ	Ann	Cert / 80%	2/1/2020	Community College Course
8 Exercises To Increase EQ	Ann / Mark	80%	8/1/2021	Online course – Company to pay
3. Communication Development	**Ann**	**Cert**	**1/1/2021**	**Developing better communication skills**
Dale Carnegie's Communication / Persuasion	Ann / Mark	Cert / 80%	6/1/2020	3-Day Dale Carnegie Cert Course
The art of negotiation / online	Ann / Mark	Completion	9/1/2020	Online / Company to pay

4. Persuasion / Influence	**Ann**	**Cert**	**1/1/2021**	**Developing Persuasion & Influence**
Dale Carnegie's Communication / Persuasion	Ann / Mark	Cert / 80%	6/1/2020	3-Day Dale Carnegie Cert Course
The art of negotiation / online	Ann / Mark	Completion	9/1/2020	Online / Company to pay
5. Assertiveness	**Ann**	**Assessment**	**1/1/2020**	**Developing & Understanding Assertiveness**
Monthly One On One Coaching	Mark	Assessment	7/1/2020	Assessment Improvement 15% Increase
6. Habits	**Ann**	**Cert**	**1/1/2020**	**Forming better habits**
7-Habits of Highly Effective People	Ann / Gary	Book / Coach	4/1/2020	Read book and coaching by Gary
7-Habits of Highly Effective People	Ann / Mark	Course	10/15/2020	Two Day Course

Not Started: Red   In Process: Yellow   Complete: Green

Ann was excited and ready to start attacking. I would rather have an employee that I have to hold back, than one I have to push forward. Ann was such an employee. However, over several years of working in personnel development, I have seen some of the most motivated individuals fail and for several reasons. Having the support and a foundation at home is important. This has tripped up many individuals. Our commitment is to be available to coach, support and commit to our part of the execution. Ann had a good definition and a plan on what she would live by and also what she would live for. She knows what she is reaching and driving towards, and that is important. She was now ready for the next stages, starting with execution and all the challenges that come with the process.

Chapter 3

PREPARE FOR BATTLE

The next stage of development and execution is to build a support network plan. I describe this as taking the battlefield. When using the phrase to take the battlefield, we truly mean to prepare for battle. Why would one prepare for battle at this stage? So far we have executed the process of defining what you will live by, by creating your personal Mission Statement, along with your values and principles to stand on and guide you. Also, you have developed a plan for advancing your skills within the foundational leadership traits. Chapter Two has now taught us to execute what we will live for. We do this by defining what your personal vision is, defining your goals and objectives with roadmaps built for successful execution. When an aspiring woman in leadership has done this, they see success and possibilities. They see a future that they had not seen before, and they see their value to society. This is motivating, as it should be motivating, as it lifts spirits, desires, and builds courage. But this is exactly why we teach to take the battlefield and to prepare a plan. What does that mean?

When one prepares for a battle they have to look for areas of possible setbacks, and be ready to push through. This is where perseverance and being of a resolute mind come in, as, in reality, one will be tested. Here is where I work with and teach the individual to build a support network before launching into full execution. This is important because, after the exercises in Chapter One and Chapter Two, most individuals believe in themselves and believe in the plan. They have an attitude that nothing will stop them and see no possible setbacks. Certainly we want them to be motivated. But here is where it is important to slow them up and to teach them to build a support network plan before moving ahead.

Why would building a support network plan be important before they move forward? This can be because of no matter the individual, their plan, or present supporters, they will encounter people and situations that will trip them up and ruin their spirits in their belief in themselves. Those that appear to have solid family support from siblings, friends, or spouses especially need to create a system that is far more reaching than that dynamic. Unfortunately, it is sometimes those that are close to you that state their support of your ideas early then become your detractors as you start executing. They become naysayers and believe that they are assisting you in being a devil's advocate, which is one who constantly explains why something will fail. When some items of execution take the commitment that alters time away from family, friends, or spouses, then this is when their support seems to change. When an investment is involved, this can have the same effect. This is why we teach immediately at this stage to build a support system plan that will provide support, mentoring, important feedback, encouragement, advice, and yes, even a kick in the tail if needed. This is best done by non-family members, but also by those who understand the challenges, the industry, and the climb ahead.

How do you build a support network plan? Find support? Gain an additional mentor? Share accountability? Executed while aligning with mentors and groups that are essential for one's support, but also for their mental strength for pushing through when challenges arise and naysayers start speaking what they believe is sound logic and advice. A naysayer comes as those closest to you, such as your friend, your spouse, and sometimes those that maybe do not have your best interest in mind. In my book *Leadership Lessons From Mom*, I tell the story of how my mother would tell me that "misery loves company." Which she further defined that in life you will encounter miserable people, who for no other reason than the fact that they are miserable, that they want everyone else to be miserable as well. This is part of a lesson where she taught me that you cannot convince the convinced. She educated me that when this happens, human nature wants us to work hard to change that individual's opinion, and this takes energy, time, and effort. It becomes a never-ending cycle and drains our energy, and at some point we may even want to give in. Well, this is where you need to realize that this person has convinced themselves that they are correct, so no amount of effort you will make will change their opinion and win them over. Once you recognize this is the scenario, you need to separate yourself from the argument and stand on your values and principles, as well as believe in your mission. Remember, you built your mission and values because you will live by them daily. As your values are automatically in action they have become your principles. Now you need to push through what you will live for, which is what you have stated you want and desire.

Learning from others is important. I recently went to lunch with an attorney friend of mine who is well respected in the Knoxville,

Tennessee area named Heather. Having known Heather and her reputation I would never have presumed that she had difficulty as a woman in leadership obtaining her status, and maintaining it to this day. It was Heather, having knowledge of me working on this book that stated, "You need to interview me." She declared this as she believes that it is still a man's world and that even though we may view her as one who has conquered and progressed, she encounters much resistance in her journey. In addition, she speaks to the fact that in her profession the male-dominated world still exists, along with some of the old attitudes that it is a man's profession. I mentioned to Heather that when I mentor aspiring women for leadership, that they are always so motivated to execute the lessons we teach and it is at this stage that I in reality hold them back a little. I believe it is important that they build a support network first, as when they begin to execute they will encounter resistance. Usually, and surprisingly, this resistance can come from those that are closest to the individual, so their resistance has power and impact. This can, at times, stop someone in their tracks and drain their motivation. I would estimate that 50% of those that have not built a support network allow themselves to get crushed by this resistance and then the demotivation stops them from further pursuit. Years later, they regret having let that dream go. We built our model to be proactive, knowing resistance will occur.

In speaking with Heather, she stated that early in her journey she had to adopt three strong beliefs. Number one, that her significance is not in what others perceive if she is successful or not. In the legal field others may be caught up in what they see on TV, such as a lawyer that can win, get any client off, and manipulate the facts. However, the reality is that in the legal field the facts are the facts, and for the most part cannot be changed or altered. So Heather quickly realized that as a lawyer, her role was to represent her clients to the fullest capabilities of the law, with ethics and principles intact. So at times when the facts on a case or with a client were not positive for the case, the reality was that Heather could not change them. What she could do is represent her client to the fullest based upon the facts and that is what she did. She witnessed too many in the legal field get caught up in how their perception of win or lose would drive them, and at times crush them. Unfortunately, this would drive some attorneys to cherry-pick what cases

· · · · · · · · · · · ·

Define where your significance comes from and base it upon your own values and principles.

· · · · · · · · · · · ·

they would take, as they wanted to manage the perception of being a winning attorney. Heather realized, and believed, that as long as she laid the foundation of strong values and principles that would guide her, demonstrate her integrity, and display strong ethics that her character would become her reputation, and so it has. So her first advice is to define where your significance comes from and base it upon your own values and principles.

The second belief Heather mentioned was to seek mentors that she could learn from, and rely upon. She also sought those she could mentor as she learned. No matter what level Heather was at, and even today, there are those in need of the mentoring, and still a few steps behind. Heather realized, and was surprised, on how quickly she encountered resistance as a woman in a male-dominated profession. Having been tutored with the caution of resistance on the prowl, Heather was fortunate to react quickly and worked on building a support network. She sought mentors, both male, and female, that had experience and had themselves faced adversity in their advancement. In addition, she found a few support groups of women empowerment and encouragement. Within those groups she found those she could mentor, and when she would mentor she would be surprised at how much she was still learning. Heather was cautious of her mindset, as she did not want to formulate an "us versus them" mentality in regards to men in the workforce. What Heather wanted to create was an "us with them" mentality that women can coexist and also be successful. Heather, like others, experienced push back from those close to her, some of which were the ones she believed were committed to her success and had she not had a support network outside of family and friends she may have faltered. In some ways you will need to show your close doubters that you will push forward despite their doubts.

The final belief Heather mentioned was to have belief in yourself, firmly. She mentions firmly because there will be times that if your belief is not firm, then you may allow yourself to be pushed and controlled. My mom once utilized the expression that "the moment you allow yourself to walk on eggshells there will be eggs at every turn." What this meant is that the moment you allowed yourself to be controlled or intimidated, the more it will reoccur as you will allow it, and others will witness it. Individuals that learn to intimidate learn subconsciously that it works for them, and they continue to do it. This is where Heather stated she was firmly grounded in her values and principles and utilized those as her foundation, which is exactly what they should be. A firm foundation allows you to be stable in how you approach and defend yourself. Heather mentioned that just within the last few weeks another attorney attempted to overshadow her from the male-dominant perspective and how she stood her ground. By standing her ground the other individual still attempted dominance, but soon acquiesced that his method was not working and that Heather was an attorney to be treated at the same level of competence. His behavior was modified when he realized his push back was not advancing his initiative.

So this is where we teach to build a support network before you rush out and encounter push back. In mentoring many individuals, their confidence and courage grows substantially in the early stages, but also can be easily crushed as they need a firm foundation beneath it. There are a lot of individuals that for some reason they believe that if they are somehow the devil's advocate on your plans that they are only looking out for your best interest. In reality, they are far from the truth. Certainly we should all have a trusted adviser that can ask good questions and provide solid opinions. But those individuals will support us as we move forward. A devil's advocate eventually becomes a drain on your mind and therefore will affect your motivation. At first sight of any type of setback they will utilize the moment and validate their spoken opinions and concerns. They will then seek credit for being right. The right type of mentors will work with you on any encountered setbacks and help you think of a strategy to push forward. They are encouragers, but not blind to proper planning and the weight of any setback. They are realists with your best interest in mind. More importantly they understand your final objective and goal, and have a mindset to help you achieve them.

Ann was eager, which was to be expected. It was great to see her growth and her belief in her dreams. I am a firm believer that

I would rather have to hold someone back than have to push them forward. Ann fits that category. She was enthusiastic and excited to start and get going. This is where, as her mentor, I needed to walk her through the next stage. The stage of building a support network. Ann, like most, wanted to do both at the same time. She wanted to attack her plan while she worked on building a support network. Unfortunately, what tends to happen is the individual will be forced with choices of building the support network or moving forward with the plan. Building the support network tends to be the one that is sacrificed as it is always believed they can circle back to this aspect. But sometimes this is at the point of facing some setbacks and the naysayer's voices are louder than the encouragers because they have not built enough encouragers. Certainly as the individual grabs momentum, and having some success with a support system, they can focus on the execution of their plan. But it is important to get into the process and have a comfort level to have the support that allows for vulnerability, as one will need to be vulnerable when reaching out for support.

Social / Community Involvement Group:

One type of support group to build within your network is social, or community, groups that fit and support the individual's interest. This can be one that supports women in business, and/or in leadership. But it can also be specific to some of the individual's goals. What do I mean by specifics? Support groups that are focused on servant leadership or an industry-specific group, are examples of what I mean. Another example, would be one that is focused on multi-level marketing. This can be useful if that is the field of interest of the individual. I met with Ann and left her with parameters of what to look for and then asked her to bring back some options from her research. As a mentor, I certainly have some that I may recommend, but I believe in having the individual involved as it will allow for them to learn the process, own the results, and learn how to pay it forward as they become mentors from the experience.

Ann and I met the next day. She was excited about some of the choices she discovered. We sat down and I asked her to walk through each of them with me. She had a laptop ready as she wanted to share some of what she found from the organization's website. Ann had a few choices ready based upon the parameters that I assigned to her.

"Okay," I stated. "Let us review what you came up with."

Ann positioned the laptop so that she and I could see the screen as it was placed between us. "I found a few groups, some for specifics and others for leadership or specific to women in leadership." She stated.

"Great," I stated. "Let's see them."

Ann went to a website that was for one of the local community colleges. The website page was from their Continuing Education Department for students striving for careers. The name of the group was 'Student Career Support Group.' This sounded very supportive. Such a group was required to serve the needs of their students who are striving for a career. I asked Ann to move to their Mission Statement for us to review. This is always an important part as we defined Ann's Mission, Vision, and Values in Steps 1 & 2. We did this to define Ann's foundation for everything she builds, in her life, her leadership, and any future business. Their Mission Statement was, *To Provide A Future Through Education*. This was a solid Mission Statement and defines the groups' intent well. What I liked about the mission was that it can be used to describe many different scenarios for the diversity of each student and each varying situation of their background and environment. They listed their values as *Integrity, Future Focused, Transparent, Challenging, and Growth Oriented.* Once again, we gave our approval of these values, especially for a community college. I liked how they spoke of being growth-oriented, as well as challenging and future-focused. Transparency is always a strength of an organization and integrity is always an imperative. I asked Ann her thoughts on each, the Mission Statement and their values. She stated that their mission was in alignment with her personal Mission Statement, *To seek solutions and betterment of myself and others through compassion and effort, and to face the future with an optimistic outlook.* She truly believed her Mission Statement, along with their values were in alignment with her personal values *of Respect, Trust, Fun, Passion, Initiative, Accountability, and Hunger.* To her, accountability matched up with the challenging aspect of their values, and both her mission and their values are future-focused. This was an important aspect as to whether she chose them as part of a support network or utilized them for other resources in the future. Ann had predetermined that they were a match. Remember, defining what she would live by was the foundation of what directs Ann's decisions. This becomes an automatic and valuable mindset as one encounters organizations, people, and resources in the future.

Ann was ready to show me the next organization she researched. This was an organization, a non-profit, designed to help support women in leadership and business. It sounded like something that could be a good match. The name was Our Empowering

Women Organization of the local city. Their Mission Statement was *To Empower Women For Growth In Developing Their Skills and Knowledge For The Betterment Of Society*. Once again, a solid Mission Statement can be utilized to define different scenarios from different stages of an individual's life and circumstance. They stated that women have natural gifts and traits, that when developed further, advances their abilities in strong and balanced decision-making, leadership, and resourcefulness. This is everything that I would preach, as women exhibit traits essential for strong, balanced leaders. Their values were listed as *Work-Life Balance, Ethics, Resolute, Perseverance, Supportive, and Fun*. I once again asked Ann to evaluate their Mission Statement and Values to define if they were in alignment, or had a possible conflict with hers. She took a few minutes, as at first, she did not see any corresponding words that matched her mission or values. I asked if that was important.

• • • • • • • • • • •

Women exhibit traits essential for strong, balanced leaders.

• • • • • • • • • • •

"No, because I do not see anything that conflicts with my Mission Statement and Values," she answered.

"That is a key point," I told her. "That is what you must evaluate first. Is there conflict within their Mission Statement and Values with yours, and if not, then is their Mission Statement and Values able to sit on the foundation of your Mission Statement and Values?"

As she thought about it, she read each of them to herself one by one. "I believe the Mission Statement does sit well on the foundation of my Mission Statement. They do not conflict, which I understand could cause problems at some point if they do," she replied.

Ann made a great point, as sometimes an individual may want something to work so bad that even if there is conflict, they will still make the choice of incorporating it within their decision, and this can have consequences at some point. If and when consequences occur, they can stop a person's progress dead in their tracks and many times can cause damage that is costly, as well as create time loss.

"What about their values, can they sit on top of the foundation of your personal values?" I asked.

Ann reviewed them, and while nodding her head yes, answered, "I believe they are a fit and a good match to sit on top of the foundation of my values. They do not conflict in any way and what I like is that they sprout out more from my foundation."

"That is a good point, Ann," I acknowledged. "Many times an individual may believe they have to be the same. What is necessary, however, is they do not conflict. Then it is positive if they allow for growth as they stay in alignment with yours. For example, perseverance is an awesome value. But as you learn to persevere, as long as it is aligned with your value of trust and respect, then it allows for growth."

Ann nodded in agreement. "One thing I appreciated is they had some testimonials on their website from members that speak of the roadblocks they encountered, and how the support of the members and mentors helped them stay focused on their goals, and even assisted with solutions to overcome the roadblocks. There were several that spoke of this and this is exactly what I need in a support group."

"Sounds like they understand that this is important and of value to their membership," I recognized. "This may be because their niche is developed around assisting women. Maybe they have a better understanding of the challenges that may arise?"

Ann was excited about what she had presented so far. However, she had a couple more, as I challenged her to find a handful, so she can then devise a plan. Many times, when walking someone through the process, we discover several resources that are a fit in some way. But then we will take the steps at deciding what works now. Many times some of the other choices are set aside for future endeavors, and for mentoring others as well. It is amazing how our knowledge grows as we research.

Chamber of Commerce / Networking Groups:

Ann had visited a few of the local Chamber of Commerce Groups. Most cities have at least one Chamber of Commerce. But it is not unusual for cities to have more than one, and ours did. They had one for the northern part of the city, as well as one for the whole city. There was one targeted for Hispanic owned businesses and another for African-American owned businesses. Ann was Hispanic, so she chose to check that one out, as well as the one targeted for the northern part of the city since our business was already a part of that Chamber. Now, Ann was not starting her own business, so visiting a Chamber of Commerce was not with the intent of her joining as a new business, but to identify what programs they may have available that would benefit her. Certainly the networking events offer great resources to meet other business sources and prospects. They have informational breakfast, lunch and dinner meetings that provide great resources of learning and expanding on your strengths and weaknesses. Some make it personal, with building programs that reach the individual members, as well as the business membership as a whole.

"I researched three different Chamber of Commerce functions, from different Chambers," Ann began.

"Very good," I replied. "Let's see what you have."

Ann listed on the board, Hispanic Chamber of Commerce. She continued, "Let me line out some things I identified and then I will go over them."

"Okay," I answered.

She wrote, Mission Statement followed by their Mission Statement. She then wrote Values and listed their values underneath. Next, she wrote out Pros & Cons with a line drawn vertically separating the words so she could list them in an obvious manner, showing what the pros and what the cons were of the specific chamber. Finally, she wrote a list down each column.

Hispanic Chamber

<u>Mission Statement</u>: To elevate the local community through leadership and business acumen, with a focus on minority development and success.

Values:	Pros:	Cons:
Involvement	Focused on Hispanic	Maybe not open enough
Investment	Good mentors available	Concerned about pride
Ethics & Trust	Financial workshops	Lacked frequency
Courage	Talks about accountability	Distance
Vision	Cost	

It was evident Ann did thorough research. She turned around to ask if I wanted her to go through each of them. I suggested she write the research of the other Chambers so we could compare them all.

"Okay," she stated, as she turned back to look at her notes and continued to write.

The Greater Chamber of Commerce

<u>Mission Statement</u>: To Create Economic Prosperity Through Leadership

Values:	Pros:	Cons:
Education	Whole city reach	Lacks niche targeting
Community Involvement	Large Companies	Large Companies
Corporate Responsibility	Small groups programs	Pertinent topics
Integrity	Successful leaders	Heavy male leaders
Focus		

The North Chamber

<u>Mission Statement</u>: To Lead The Way For Others To Gain Success

Values:	Pros:	Cons:
Initiative	Targeted	Maybe too large
Professionalism	Many programs	Cost
Accountability	Mentors	Time of events
Trust / Integrity	Strong Foundations	
Individually Focused	Small, mid & large companies	

Ann finished writing and took a moment to analyze her notes while she was reviewing the whiteboard. "I believe that is it," she said.

"Looks like you gathered good information. Good job!" I congratulated. "Okay, walk through one at a time, and explain your comments as well as the thoughts behind them."

Ann sighed to take a moment for her thoughts. "Okay, here it is. The first chamber listed is the Hispanic Chamber. As you can see their Mission Statement is *To elevate the local community through leadership, business acumen, with a focus on minority development and success.* I know you will ask how that aligns with my personal Mission Statement of *To seek solutions and betterment of myself and others through compassion and effort and to face the future with an optimistic outlook."*

"Absolutely," I agreed. "You know we want to make sure the alignment with your foundation is there. So I believe the key question of your Mission Statement is do the others align that they make you better, and do they demonstrate compassion? How does each organization align in helping build a future with an optimistic outlook?"

"Good question," Ann replied. "I believe that is more than just the mission aligning, but also the values along with the whole organization."

"You are correct," I answered. "As it usually is always more than one key point. Also, sometimes each organization may be in alignment. But you will find one that aligns more than others, and sometimes that is based on what stage of growth you are in at the time."

Ann continued, "I do like the mission of developing business acumen as I have a desire for my betterment. To affect the community through leadership demonstrates compassion as well. So in that regards it does align with my mission. More importantly, it does not misalign."

"Sounds like you thought it through correctly," I observed. It is important that if there were more questions or considerations that Ann did not think of, that I, as a mentor, bring them out. This is an important factor because when we mentor others we teach them how to mentor. This allows them to pay it forward. "What are your thoughts on their values?" I asked Ann. "Anything stick out as positives? Or is there anything that is a concern for you?"

Ann paused for a moment, "I believe their values are a good foundation. I like the investment aspect. Investment of time, money, and educating others is what they speak about on their website. I do appreciate that, and it matches having compassion for improving oneself and others. The involvement is a value of being involved. Ethics and trust are common values, and you would hope that every organization puts that as a foundation. Courage is a solid value to place forward. This encourages others to take bold steps and to push forward in growing and in making the right decisions. Vision is one that I like, as we all believe that great leaders and great organizations need to have a solid vision, as well as to share it with others."

"Yes," I agreed. "They are all solid values. Obviously for them to be principles they need to be automatic in action. That is the true test of principles."

Ann nodded her head in agreement. "I know some members of their chamber and they speak well of the organization. That is what I know of them."

"Sometimes how people speak of an organization is very enlightening especially if it is unsolicited," I encouraged. "Walk me through your pros and cons."

"Okay." Ann moved towards the whiteboard. "Here are the pros as I saw them. I like that they are focused on Hispanics as they have an understanding of our mentality, as well as our beliefs. Sometimes understanding our upbringing and the challenges we face add tremendous value."

"What are the drawbacks that you see to that?" I asked.

Ann responded, "I wrote that in my cons. One is maybe their focus is too narrow. Not sure how that plays out, but it was a concern. Besides, in some of the things I read, I noticed a hint of rising up out of pride. There was a statement about being held back because of being Hispanic, which I do not agree with. I am cautious about what I call victim-hood. There is a difference in recognizing roadblocks and barriers and working to overcome them rather than believing that I am entitled to something because of being a victim. I appreciate that what I have learned and what we teach our leaders here is to speak like a leader and not a victim. So that creates a concern if I hear or read examples of this."

"Talk to me about the rest of the pros that you listed," I urged.

"Sure," Ann continued. "Because I already know several members and have knowledge of many of the companies associated, I recognize good mentors available. They speak about accountability within their organizations but also workshops on accountability, which sounds exactly like something beneficial. They also have a couple of different financial workshops available, which matches my list of personal and professional goals. Workshops that teach me business finances and advances my areas of knowledge for personal finance are of tremendous value. The final pro was that cost was within reason, even for the workshops. As cost could be a concern."

"Sounds like a good list of pros," I commented. "What about the rest of the cons?"

Ann pointed to the last two items under her cons list on the whiteboard. "Well, good workshops, but the frequency was only once per quarter. So if you miss one you have to wait. My concern is, things can happen, which takes you away and that focus can be lost. The final con I noted is the distance to where the chamber meets and holds their workshops. This is a concern, as sometimes schedules get tight and do not always go as planned."

I further inquired, "Do any of your cons listed outweigh your pros, that you would eliminate this as a choice?"

Ann stayed silent and thought for a moment. "No, I like many of the things they offer. If I choose to move forward, I now know what commitment I would have to make. Especially with the cost and the distance."

"Great," I replied. "So let's walk through the next chamber and your notes."

Ann pointed to her next chamber listed. "The Greater Chamber of Commerce," she stated. "Their Mission Statement is: To Create Economic Prosperity Through Leadership. Which in some ways sounds confusing to me."

"In what way?" I asked.

"Maybe it is just too plain or too simplistic. I struggle to see specifics in it. Something that describes what, how, and why? Maybe if they expanded on it by stating 'through leadership development and spreading of knowledge through education.' That at least helps me to understand more. So to me, their Mission Statement is confusing. I remember you teaching me, that a Mission Statement should demonstrate how it benefits the individual as well as the organizations it serves."

> . . . .
>
> *A Mission Statement should demonstrate how it benefits the individual as well as the organizations it serves.*
>
> . . . .

"Very good points, Ann." I was pleased to hear Ann's insight as she had a good grasp of logic and reasoning that was demonstrated through her thought process. "Walk me through their values and your thoughts."

Ann responded, "I did not see anything majorly wrong with their values, as they have value and can be a good foundation. I am just not sure if they constructed their values for their organization to live by, or if they constructed their values for show. Something that looks good to those they are seeking to attract."

"Interesting," I mused. "Tell me, how did you come to those conclusions?"

Ann took a breath as if to gather her thoughts. "I think it started when I read their Mission Statement and tried to make sense of it. It sounds simple and sexy, but to me, that is it. It does not show how it benefits me. So the values listed sound like they may be what they believe corporate America wants to hear, and it appears like that is who they are attracting. They seem to be built with large organizations, which most of them, because of their size, are a part of more than one chamber. So I am not sure if something is lost in not having mid-level and small companies included."

"Expand on that some more?" I pushed. "Give me some examples."

"Well, when I read about what they do, they certainly state they do community involvement, but it seems these are more from large corporate initiatives and large organized drives. These things are good, like United Way Drives and other programs. They are good programs, but the other two chambers had initiatives where they touched the community directly, by serving directly. It was just a different level of involvement. So their values drive what a large organization might be involved in. I have nothing against this, I just wonder if it's for me at this stage."

"So what did the pros and cons tell you?" I asked.

"It confirmed some of my beliefs that I just stated," she said. "They obviously have a whole city reach, which they tout as a positive, and which it certainly can be. But with a city our size it might be too large and it limits having a niche as they have to be all things to all people, in a manner of speaking."

"Good points, explain more?" I urged.

Ann responded, "Well, you can see where I list large companies as a pro and as a con. So this is where I stated there are benefits, but drawbacks regarding that. I also listed as a pro that they have small group programs, but as a con the topics are more targeted for larger company personnel. Finally, I like the fact that with large companies, you have industry leaders involved who would be great to learn from. I am not sure how involved they are. My final con was the organization is heavy male. In looking at their member's list, the members are 75% male as I would estimate. As we know, even with the Fortune 1000 only 5% to 8% of CEOs are women. So if the chamber is of large companies, this also gives weight to the membership. Just having more women would provide me a little more comfort."

"Ann, these are all great observations," I commented. "Sounds like this one may not be for you at this time. If, as you grow and possibly work for a larger company, you may see a time where this choice makes sense and can come back to it."

"Thanks, Mark," she replied. "It just did not seem right for me at this time. This exercise helped demonstrate that to me. I can't imagine where some people join without researching, and they are caught in the middle, having invested. I appreciate the process."

"Thanks," I responded. "Let's walk through the last chamber."

"Okay," Ann continued. "The North Chamber. Their Mission Statement is *To Lead The Way For Others To Gain Success*. I like the Mission Statement. When I ask if this benefits me, I can see that it correlates to me. It matches the motto of paying it forward and teaching each other. I found this enlightening when I first read it."

"Good, and their values?"

"Initiative is a strong value out of the gate," Ann remarked. "Initiative matches the word effort in my Mission Statement. It signifies stepping out with courage. Then with professionalism as the second value, I like as it just sets a standard. It lays a solid foundation to build upon. These are followed by having account-ability as the third value, which sets the stage as we hold ourselves and each other accountable. In fact, I believe that thought was given to the order in which their values are listed. Initiative, with professionalism, and accountability, are prime examples to demon-strate to members what the chamber stands for and what they will provide to their members."

I nodded my head in agreement, "I can see that as well. They had a very good thought process on how they built their values."

"I thought so. Theirs captured me in a positive way, where the prior one just confused me," Ann concurred. "This is why I like how they completed their values with trust, integrity, and individ-ually focused. The individually focused portion adds excitement as they are stating that they take a focus on you individually, which adds value. I definitely believe and see where this is in alignment with my values."

"Sounds like they made a good impression," I emphasized. "Walk me through the pros and cons along with your thoughts."

Ann seemed enthusiastic. "Once again, the pros are easy to define, and most are listed as their benefits to their membership on their website. The word targeted details that they have programs and a philosophy to define what their members need, as well as to define ways to provide the resources. This is shown by the many programs that they have, which include live workshops as well as online courses provided, so one can take advantage of both. They speak of a mentor program that you can join groups, but also request a mentor for certain topics and needs."

"That sounds like they really want to make an impact with each member," I commented.

"It does and this chamber excites me," Ann said with elation. "I wrote strong foundations as to me it is evident with their Mission Statement and their Values provides a strong foundation for everything that they do."

"How do small, mid and large companies fit within the pros section?"

"They break this down on their website. One, it allows for small organizations to work with others their size about similar situations they may have, mid-size and large size organizations as well. But they are speaking to the fact that as your organization is growing, you have the availability and mentorship of organizations larger than yours that have been through the growth struggles and overcame the adversity. Whom better to listen to? This adds value."

"Yes, I certainly agree with you!" I exclaimed. "How about the cons, are they concerning enough to make you have thoughts against joining any of their programs?"

Ann spoke up, "You can see I only listed three. I wrote it may be too large. But as I assessed things further I see they break down their support to where you are not lost in the shuffle. Cost is a factor, as some appealing items cost, and that may be a challenge. The final one is the time of events. This means that several things are scheduled at the time that I am at work. There are things in the evening as well, but the challenge will be when there is something that conflicts with my work schedule."

"I understand," I replied. "But that may be an item that you take one step at a time if you believe the value of their offerings brings high-level benefit. Is this something you would state?"

"Yes," Ann answered, quickly. "I would state that their programs and mentorships excite me. "It would disappoint me if a roadblock prevented me from benefiting."

"Great, so our next stage is to map out which ones you align with for your support network and how you take the steps."

"Sounds like a plan," Ann agreed.

I instructed Ann to study each and create an outline of what she believed would be the correct choices and why. I coached Ann to list out what would be next in regards to each support group, as well as to list if there is an order of sequence or if they overlap and can be completed at the same time. I informed her that I would be interested in her thoughts and what drove her decisions. She understood. I left the room for a conference call and let her know I would be back in approximately 45-minutes.

Defining A Support Network:

Ann and I met back again to work on building her support network. Key items in building a support network are to choose those that will allow you to be vulnerable and will help you with self-account-ability. As mentioned before, the caution is where an individual might gravitate towards staying in a comfort zone and choosing from friends and family who have committed to support us in our endeavors. My advice is to push yourself outside your comfort zone and find your support network from outside resources other than friends and family. This allows several benefits. The first benefit as I previously stated is that it is usually those closest to you that become your first challenge in supporting your efforts. Because your effort usually affects your habits, routines, and lifestyle, that at the moment you

> *Push yourself outside your comfort zone and find your support network from resources other than friends and family.*

move forward is when those close to you will resist the change and become less supportive. Also, by choosing outside resources you will expand your experiences as well as expand your learning with new ideas, perspectives, approaches, and knowledge. When you build accountability, there is less emotion when assisting in holding you accountable and the coaching received from mentors is more factual while holding your best interest in mind.

I could see Ann had worked on fleshing out her choices. She had erased the whiteboard and created a list of items in which she categorized as *Immediate Needs*. She then listed out what she believed her needs would be from a support network.

The list on the board looked like this:

Immediate Needs

Accountability Partner	To be challenged
Mentor	Camaraderie
Emotional Support	Access to experience
Insight of others	Different levels of knowledge
Stability & Consistency	Different level of skills

"I can see that you gave it some thought," I noted. "Tell me about what you have listed on the board."

Ann walked over to the list on the board and raised her hand to point to what was written. "In thinking about the process, and with the seven habits of highly effective people in mind, I started thinking about what is the end in mind? What does success look like with the right support network, and what are the traits that would be in those groups or individuals that would drive me to success?"

"Very good," I replied. "I appreciate the way you gave it some thought, to help draw out the best options." In my mind I was very pleased with the effort and the way Ann was thinking things through. It demonstrated her growth. "Please proceed Ann."

"Okay," Ann began. "When we discussed a support network and what role they would play, it became important that I separate the support I believe I need and realize this may be different than the specific knowledge I will pursue, which could be from the same resource, but not necessarily."

Ann paused and looked at me for acknowledgment. I nodded in agreement and allowed her to proceed. She continued, "Here is where I went one by one on what I believe my needs are. I pushed myself to look and expand outside my comfort zone, which I must admit is a bit scary. So, the first thing I need is to define a specific accountability partner. I know that within the groups there will be accountability. But an accountability partner, as we do here, where it is one specific person that I meet with monthly and where we would streamline the process to build accountability. I would share with my accountability partner my plans for the next 30-days, as well as my long-term plan. This will allow them to monitor and measure if I am making progress. Each month we can measure my progress against milestones built into the long-term plans, and I can also list three monthly goals that I wish to achieve, broken down in three separate categories. Goal one would be what I will accomplish for professional development, so it could be learning something new at work like a new skill or new knowledge that benefits my employer. Goal two would be specific to what I will accomplish for personal development, like educating myself with reading or taking something online, which advances my skills or knowledge for personal benefit. The third goal would be something task-oriented that has a measurement of achievement. This will assist in developing myself in being held accountable at goals that have specific measurements."

"That is a good mindset," I complimented her. "We could redesign our worksheet for an accountability partner to assist you in this format. Let's make sure we do that, so you will have something physical that you fill out and share with your accountability partner. This allows a documented process."

Ann nodded in agreement. "That would be useful. Especially when I start mentoring others too. You see my next item is the need for a mentor. Now certainly this can be more than one mentor, as each may have varying knowledge or skill levels. But as we discussed, it is beneficial to have one lead mentor at a time that I rely on for the bulk of my mentoring."

I raised my right hand to make a point and to capture Ann's attention. "It is important that you find a mentor that leads with humility, as that is an important aspect for any leader within your belief system. Humility, I believe, allows the mentor to be transparent, and also allows for two way vulnerability between you and the mentor. Which will add tremendous value to both parties. Remember the best mentors understand that they will learn from those they mentor and with each mentoring experience."

Ann listened carefully and asked, "Can you break down for me what you mean by allowing for vulnerability?"

"Sure," I replied. "When I make the statement about allowing for vulnerability, what I mean is to allow the ability, and the comfort level, to ask anything, or to bring up any situation that in other circumstances you may be embarrassed or shy about. This is actually a trust factor that you and the mentor develop, and most mentors realize this. You need the ability to believe that there is no such thing as a stupid question, and in regards to those within your support network that there is no situation that is too embarrassing. You need the ability to bring up anything. But I also will advise you that you need to demonstrate that you are learning from such situations and that you can take control."

"I understand," Ann stated, "The caution here is to not sound or come across too needy."

"I agree," I stated, nodding my head. "That is why I state that you will need to demonstrate that you learn from each experience, as a good mentor will define and coach you with this in mind."

"That makes sense," Ann contemplated. Ann started laughing a little while speaking. "Well, next is where I list emotional support, but not where I am too needy like we just discussed. However, I realize and believe that there will be challenges. Possibly some challenges that I have not even considered. So having a support system for encouragement and emotional support will be important. I am sure there will be circumstances that others have already experienced and have overcome. So having this type of support will help stabilize me."

"I agree one hundred percent," I declared, as I pounded my hand on the table. "There is nothing more powerful than to be supported with those that have already been there and fought through it."

"Yes, I agree." Ann turned back to the whiteboard. "The next item listed is the insight of others. So not just my direct mentor or mentors, but I am sure at times there may be a subject where another member may have more expertise. To have that available would be valuable and a luxury." Ann looked towards me to see if I had any comments.

"Explain to me stability and consistency," I questioned.

Ann paused for a moment. "By listing stability and consistency here is what I meant. By reviewing each group and organization, there was some indication that a group or two had constant changes, or lacked consistency in what they deliver to their members. Even the turnover of personnel could be an issue. One chamber demonstrated on their website long-term employees and long-term members. That gives me comfort."

"I think it is smart that they demonstrate their stability and consistency on their website," I replied. "But I do agree with how you define stability and consistency as an important item, so things don't all of a sudden change after you become involved. Next item, to be challenged, define that for me."

"Well, Mark, you have always taught me that the best way to grow, learn, and develop is to go outside our comfort zone. To have leaders and mentors that move us outside our comfort zone and utilize this to challenge our development. Besides, if and when setbacks happen, as they will, to be challenged to push forward and to push through the roadblock, is important. Finally, I know from experience and your leadership, that it is human nature that at times we relax in our comfort zone, and it takes leadership to recognize this and adjust our mindset. That is what I mean by listing, to be challenged."

> • • • • • • • • • • •
> *At times we relax in our comfort zone, and it takes leadership to recognize this and adjust our mindset.*
> • • • • • • • • • • •

"Okay, I understand. You want to ensure that you are challenged and taken outside your comfort zone. Very good. Next, I know what camaraderie means and I believe I have a general understanding of why you listed it. But touch on it for me to ensure I understand," I inquired.

Ann spoke, "I am sure you are aware of my belief in this area. I believe that those we work with, challenge each other with, and learn with, need to have mutual trust and friendship for it to be successful over a length of time. It is important to me that at some level, I have enjoyment from the process with those I spend time with."

Nodding my head in agreement, I smiled. "I think you summarized that well. I believe that camaraderie is important, and when achieved you advance more. On your next item listed, which is access to experience, isn't that much like the insight of others?"

"There may be some overlap, as I mentioned, but I placed this there because access to experienced individuals I believe expands on the insight of others. When I state insight of others this may be the specific group I am a part of, and many times may be somewhat on the same level that I am. So having the ability to have access to some higher level of experience, and different levels of experience would add additional value. Sometimes it may be one question or one scenario that someone from their experience can add insight to."

"Okay, I can see the difference as you explained. Would that somewhat be similar to different levels of knowledge?" I asked.

"It is in a way," Ann responded. "There is some overlap. But like experience I just wanted to flesh it out in more detail, as experience can be what an individual has been through and knowledge is what they have in a range of information and skill level. So by adding this I believe I hit on all the key points to allow me to make my assessment."

"Okay, I understand," I acquiesced. "I like your passion for how you believe the importance that you list each and include for your assessment to make your decisions. I think you just answered the final one, different level of skills, correct?"

"Yes, I did speak to it when we spoke of knowledge. Having different skill sets just adds value when I may need resources when going through a challenge, or working through a situation," Ann answered.

"Great, so let's get to the choices that you selected, and see how they line up," I stated.

"Sounds good," Ann responded. "The first thing I did was to eliminate what I believed was not a match for me at this moment. This does not mean, however, they won't be a match at some other time."

"Okay, so what did you eliminate?" I questioned.

"The first option I eliminated was the Greater Chamber of Commerce. As I stated when we reviewed their Mission Statement and Values, I saw them as confusing. In addition, with a focus on large organizations I do not see them as a match for me at this moment. Many of these large organizations, because of their size, are associated with the other chambers as well. So there is a possibility that I can still associate with many of them."

Nodding my head in agreement, "I can agree with your analysis. Now elaborate on the next one you eliminated?"

Ann continued, "I eliminated the Community College option. Now understand, this was difficult for me as I see that they are in alignment with my mission and values, but what they have to offer I believe I can obtain through one of my other choices. Furthermore, I believe that the Community College may be an option that I circle back to in the future. I certainly may take a course or two from the college, but because of what I found at one of the Chambers that match those needs and more, I eliminated this choice for now."

"Very good," I congratulated. "You can see how this exercise has value and can be difficult at moments. You found a good resource that for now you will set aside, but at another time may add value."

"Yeah," Ann said, laughing. "I certainly saw the challenge. For a moment I did not want to let go. But I realized I have to limit my bandwidth to be effective."

"Absolutely," I replied in agreement. "Your energy always needs to be focused on achievement. You will have enough on your plate with your job, things to learn, and your support network. How you manage that is important."

"Thanks, I see that," Ann acknowledged. "It was difficult. But now this brings me to what I chose. My first choice is the Our Empowering Women group. As I measured their organization with the pros and cons, as well as their mission and values, this became a choice that I believe the support would be valuable from the start. It is also an organization that I probably would stay with for a long time as I believe I would naturally gravitate as a mentor to others. But I do like the idea of women supporting women, as we can allow ourselves to be vulnerable early within the relationship. The groups they have are positive, and I believe they will make an impact. I know that if I need an accountability partner that I could find one there as well. The cost is low and reasonable as they are non-profit. This one just makes sense."

"Good choice, you will have no argument from me," I concurred. "I can see you understand your choices and why this one can benefit you from the start. Now, I did not hear that you elimi-nated another chamber, so did you choose between the other two?"

Ann responded, quickly. "No, I did eliminate one and chose the other. One factor made it difficult, but I will have to figure it out."

"What do you mean?" I inquired.

Ann sighed, took a breath and continued. "My choice is the North Chamber. With what they offer with mentors, small groups, and different size organizations, it aligns up well with my needs over the Hispanic Chamber. I will keep the Hispanic Chamber as a future option for what they offer. My only concern about the North Chamber is cost and some of the possible scheduling con-flicts of their events as well as my work schedule. But their benefits far outweigh the challenges."

"Choices are not always easy. That is part of life," I said, while laughing. "But let's take a step back. Our organization is part of the North Chamber, so you do not have to pay new fees if you go as part of our business. I will approve this because your growth, I believe, will pay dividends for our business. Now, as we line out the events that make sense for you, we can find a balance for some around work hours, but also allow for some during work hours. I will allow this as long as your duties are accomplished and planned around. We will communicate issues as they arise. Agreed?"

Ann was excited and quickly answered, "Yes, you have my commitment. But I do have one more thing to ask you."

"Okay," I replied, waiting for her question.

"I want to make sure that I will still have access to you as a mentor," Ann declared.

"Ann," I responded, as I looked in her direction. "You certainly will have me as a mentor. This will not change from my perspective.

I certainly want to see your growth. But know that I understand and recognize, that as you grow and obtain other mentors, our interaction will morph in different ways and you may not need my mentorship as much. That just means you are growing."

"I am not sure about that!" She exclaimed.

"Trust me," I replied, with a smile. "Nothing will excite me more. Now I need you to take the steps this next week to lining these two support networks up, and implementing your support network plan. Once you have taken action in this area we will meet again and finalize and adjust your development plan for execution."

"Thanks, I will get started on it right away," Ann declared.

As the next week passed, Ann took the initiative to set herself up in each group of support. Within a few weeks she was active and enjoyed the interaction and camaraderie she desired.

Document Creation:

With these meetings with Ann, and as suggested, we created documents to help support the process for future mentoring of aspiring women leaders. We created an assessment document to help assist future participants in evaluating the different support networks they will research. Also, we developed a document to support the process for defining what choices are made and what ones are eliminated. Both of the documents need to be saved for future reference and future considerations.

Mark Villareal
People, Strategy, Execution

Support Network Evaluation Form

Fill this form out for each organization, group, or individual that you are considering to include in your support network. Answer questions as thoroughly as possible giving thought to what aligns with your expected next steps, stage of growth, and your mission and values.

1. Name of organization, group, or individual:

    _____

2. List their Mission Statement / Personal Mission:

    _____

    _____

    _____

3. Define your thoughts on what their mission means to you, and what is their focus?

    _____

    _____

    _____

    _____

4. Explain how their mission can be a benefit to you?

    _____

    _____

    _____

    _____

5. List out the Values or Principle Statements:

_____

_____

_____

_____

_____

6. Describe your assessment of their values or principles. Do they make sense and are they a good foundation?

_____

_____

_____

_____

_____

7. Do you believe their values or principles are in alignment with yours, or is there any conflict?

_____

_____

_____

_____

_____

8. List out what you define are the pros with this potential support opportunity. Describe:

_____

_____

_____

_____

_____

9. List out what you define are the cons with this potential support opportunity. Describe:

_____

_____

_____

_____

10. Does this support opportunity align with your goals & objectives, and stage that you are at?

_____

_____

_____

_____

Mark Villareal
People. Strategy. Execution

Support Network Selection Form

Answer and fill out the sections below in regards to what types of support that will assist you in your growth and learning. This is different than what skills and knowledge you desire to learn, as that will be part of a development plan.

The definition of a support group is 'a group of individuals who meet regularly to assist and support each other for morale, encouragement, share experiences, discuss challenges, and provide empathy, and accountability as a safety net for each member.'

At your current stage of development and experience with a support network and mentors, circle no more than six items from the list below what you define as your current needs:

Empathy	Encouragement	Insight
Experience	Knowledge	Skill Level
Accountability	Mentorship	Need Mentors
To be challenged	Vulnerability	Morale
Acceptance	Evaluation	Sympathy
Strategy	Burden Sharing	Camaraderie
Consistency	Stability	Intellectual Stimulation

What, if anything, in addition to the list that you circled, do you believe you need and why?

_____

_____

_____

_____

List out below each item that you circled and define why you chose that option, and how you believe it will assist you in your development.

1. _____:

2. _____:

3. _____:

4. _____:

5. _____:

*Utilize this form with a mentor to help select your support network groups or organization.

Chapter 4

OVERCOMING OBSTACLES: SUPPORT NETWORK IMPLEMENTATION

Ann was excited about building her foundation of support. I reminded her, as I did often, to build the foundation of support, stabilize the methods, and then start implementing her execution on personal and professional goals. It is common when mentoring an individual at this stage that they are so excited and determined, that they believe nothing can stop them. Which isn't a bad thing to believe. However, without the foundation built and stable, the first roadblock will halt their progress and deflate that feeling of invincibility. It was important for me to ensure Ann took the proper steps to build the foundation. We agreed we would meet once per week, at a minimum, and review her progress. Should an individual not wait until the foundation is built and stable, when they encounter push back and roadblocks, they falter. When they eventually get back on track, they have lost valuable time and momentum. Also, I firmly believe that when an individual takes the proper steps to build the foundation and allows the proper time for stability to set in, that individual saves time so that when the momentum sets in they accomplish things at a steady pace.

Ann and I met, and she was eager to get started. I asked her, "What are your first steps?" as I wanted to ensure it was what we had already discussed and there were no surprises.

"The plan is still the same," Ann stated. "I have a meeting tomorrow with a member of Our Empowering Women to sign up and get started. They sent some materials and questionnaires for me to fill out and send back today that we will review in our meeting."

Ann showed me some of the questionnaires on her laptop. There were the obvious ones for her name and history on her work development. But there were also in-depth materials that would allow them some insight on Ann's goals, past failures, and her outlook and perspective on life. I was pleased and impressed with the materials and it provided comfort that Ann discovered a good program. I asked her to give me insight after her meeting. She agreed.

Meeting with Our Empowering Women:

Ann arrived at the small office of Our Empowering Women. She met with an individual named Sally whose title was Members Liaison. Sally was a very pleasant, middle-aged lady in professional appearance. She had a folder, with a handbook, and she also had Ann's information that she filled out the previous day and sent back in via email.

"Ann," Sally greeted her. "I am so excited to meet with you today. I reviewed your materials and we believe that you would be a great addition to our organization."

"Thank you," replied Ann. "I did research before deciding, as I believe in what you offer, as well as what I can provide as a member are a good match."

"I agree," concurred Sally. "I, in fact, appreciate some of your answers and insight into your goals, as they are specific, which demonstrates your focus."

"Thanks," replied Ann. "I have a good boss, who is a good mentor. So he has worked with me on SMART Goals, Values and Principles, and even my Missions Statement and Vision Statement." Ann pulled out from a leather satchel the examples she built of her Principle, Mission, and Vision Statements.

"Can I see those?" Sally asked.

Ann handed them to Sally, "Sure, here."

Sally looked over them slowly, making small comments as she read them to herself. You could tell that Sally was captivated by the contents and structure.

"Ann," Sally continued. "I really like how you structured these. It is evident you put your heart into it and gave it some deep thought."

"Thanks," Ann responded. "As I mentioned, my Vice President, who is a mentor to me, walked me through the process and even challenged me during the process as well. He expressed how important this would be as a foundation for me moving forward. He expressed and explained how every future decision I make, in life, as well as in a career, should point back to my values, principles, mission, and vision. So they are not only a foundation for stability, but also a guide for direction."

Sally was impressed. She could already foresee that Ann would be a good addition and add value to the organization. "Ann, this is something I would like to not only share with the other members, but add to our organization on what we teach other members. I certainly could see you being instrumental in teaching these sessions."

Ann was surprised, but also excited. "I would love that opportunity! In fact, my Vice President is always teaching that as we learn it is important to pay it forward and mentor others. He teaches that as you mentor others, you will be amazed at how much you learn from those you mentor."

"Exactly, I know what you mean," Sally replied, excitedly. "I know that the more I mentor I not only learn from those I mentor, but I also develop better communication and leadership skills."

Ann nodded her head in agreement. "Yes, one of the items my boss helped me assess is not only my leadership traits, but also my emotional intelligence. Here are some copies of those assessments."

Sally was handed the assessments from Ann and her eyes grew larger as she perused what was handed her. "Wow, these are awesome. I certainly see how you will not only contribute, but quickly become a leader in our organization. Thanks for sharing these."

Ann was excited and had gained a quick comfort level with Sally and the organization. Besides, her confidence in herself and her knowledge expanded as well. She had heard the reassurance from her Vice President, but hearing from an outside resource provided additional insight.

Sally started speaking again, "Ann, this is our handbook, which covers a solid foundation of who we are. However, instead of just handing it to you and assigning you to read it. I want to walk you through a few pages of importance and then speak of how you will need to review it."

"Okay," Ann replied, while moving closer to see.

Sally opened the handbook, and the first thing listed was the organization's Mission Statement. "To Empower Women for Growth in Developing Their Skills and Knowledge for the Betterment of Society," Sally read out loud. "This is the Mission Statement of our organization. By sharing your values and principles, along with your mission and vision, I can see that this benefits you by helping you achieve your mission, and strive towards your vision. Also, we are committed to providing resources that further help develop your skills and your knowledge that assist in your growth personally as well as professionally. What is also important in our organization, is to support each other through mentoring, and encouragement, as well as accountability."

Ann was impressed by how Sally was presenting the information. "This is one of the things I appreciated about your organization. Your listing of your Mission Statement and your marketing outreach on your website demonstrates that it is more than just words."

"I like to think so," agreed Sally. "I have been with the organization six-years and the passion for helping women grow and develop has always been high. Also, we are always looking to include more innovative ways to become stronger and provide more."

"I appreciated many of the testimonials that were on your website," Ann added. "The messages were consistent, from women of all levels."

"Thank you," Sally commented. "This is why we place such an emphasis on our values, to make sure they provide a good foundation and are more than words." Sally flipped another page to showcase the values of Our Empowering Women. "Here are the values, Work-Life Balance, Ethics, Resolute, Perseverance, Supportive, and Fun. Note the bookends of work-life balance and fun, add action and commitment to the others."

Ann responded. "Yes, I reviewed them thoroughly to ensure they do not conflict with mine, in which they do not. But more importantly, do they add value to the actions described in your mission, and everything else about your organization. This excited me about the organization."

"I am impressed by your thoroughness," Sally replied, with wonder.

"This was part of what my mentor taught me," Ann answered.

"I can see that you have a smart mentor," Sally acknowledged. "I am sure you already know that."

"I do," Ann beamed. "I do let him know that I appreciate his mentorship."

"It is important that you do," Sally commented. "Good mentors are hard to find, so we must let them know we value them." Sally continued through the beginning portion of the handbook. "Can I ask about some of your goals and immediate needs?"

"Sure," Ann answered. Ann handed Sally a piece of paper which had the small chart of immediate needs she had worked with her Vice President on.

Sally reviewed the list. "Accountability Partner, To be challenged, Mentor, Camaraderie, Emotional Support, Access to experience, Insight of others, Different levels of knowledge, Stability & Consistency, and Different levels of skills. These are all very good. I would like to keep this list in your file, so you and I can review to see how we are providing for these."

"Sounds reasonable to me," Ann replied. "However, that list was for any place I seek support from. Some places may only provide some of those resources, but all of them together should provide each."

"I understand," answered Sally. "However, in looking at them, I believe we can supply each at different levels. So if you have any other organization that can do the same, it only makes those areas more complete. Here is what I recommend. Read these next two portions of the workbook. The first portion is pages 4 to 8, and the second portion is pages 9 to 12. Let's schedule a time where we can speak by phone or video chat the next two nights going over portion one tomorrow and portion two the day after tomorrow."

Ann agreed. She and Sally scheduled for the same time each day over the next two days and agreed on video chat. Ann sent Sally a calendar invite from her cell phone where she had access to her email.

"Great," Sally finished. "After that, then let's walk through your needs and outline the priorities and fit what we can into what we provide.

"Sounds good," Ann responded. They hugged and each left walking towards their vehicles.

Ann enjoyed the meeting and appreciated how Sally went through the workbook as demonstrating value and understanding what was important to her. This was evident and spoke volumes of the organization.

The next evening video call:

Ann and Sally started their call at the scheduled time the next day. The pages they reviewed, pages 4 through 8, covered the meetings and sessions the organization would have scheduled and their purpose. Sally walked Ann through and discussed their bi-weekly meetings and their purpose of meeting new members, reviewing the organization's objectives, and setting goals. The monthly sessions were held on Saturdays and were scheduled for six-hours in length. The organization would provide lunch, and the sessions would always provide a presenter, who would educate on certain topics to add value to the members. The additional time would be allocated to break down future meeting content, and they would end with discussing additional membership needs to add.

Ann appreciated the insight and the ability to ask Sally questions for clarity when needed. She could see that the organization took planning seriously, and wanted each member to have an understanding so they could provide insight and be prepared.

The next evening Sally and Ann went over pages 9 through 12. These pages had Ann's attention and she was prepared with questions for Sally. These pages covered sessions, seminars, webinars, and eLearning that was available within the membership for educational purposes, support and coaching, as well as accountability and goal achievement. Ann could see the value and alignment with many of her needs. She could also foresee where she could play a role in adding value.

"Here is where I would like us to select one to three items from what we reviewed and schedule them out for you," announced Sally.

"That sounds great," Ann replied. "I have a pretty good idea. I may have a question or two, though."

Ann and Sally discussed the different sessions and scheduled two of them. They would be in person on alternating Tuesday evenings. One Tuesday would be one session on one topic, and the alternating Tuesday would be on another topic. Ann did find an eLearning course on finances she selected, that she could do at her own pace.

She was excited, but still needed to understand the flow of each session. She was set to attend the membership standard meeting to be introduced and meet others. She found it unusual that she was a little nervous. As she wants to make a good impression.

The membership biweekly meeting arrived and Ann showed up early. Everyone was so welcoming, and she had good vibes from the members. The meeting started and the current members introduced themselves describing their journey and growth. It was very inspiring. It truly encouraged Ann. Soon it was Ann's turn to speak. She introduced herself and told her story of having a desire to grow and develop, as well as provide more for her family. She described being mentored and the desire to pay it forward. Sally spoke up during Ann speaking and mentioned how impressed she was with Ann when they initially met, and how Ann had her values, principles, mission, and vision all defined. The attendees seemed to appreciate the topic as one committee member stated they would like Ann to possibly hold a session teaching others how to do the same. That idea excited Ann. She mingled and made new friends. She started attending the regular meeting along with her additional sessions and looked forward to each one. Ann recognized her growth and could see this was a good choice.

Over time, Ann was able to define skill sets and knowledge of others that she valued and sought to learn from. In addition, others recognized Ann for her skill sets and gravitated towards her for their needs that Ann could assist with. Soon Ann was holding a session or two on topics she had been mentored on. She appreciated what she had been taught and demonstrated that appreciation by paying it forward. As Ann made friends with members, there was a natural environment of encouragement and support. Ann witnessed and supported others at times when they sought counsel, or just needed someone to listen. Ann had found a newly added level of support that was different from home life as it was other women like her that had walked the path, was starting to walk the path, or was farther down the path already. Ann found a place where she belonged.

Within a few weeks, Ann selected an Accountability Partner and implemented what she was taught from her mentor. The organization asked Ann to teach others about an Accountability Partner, and they held a session for all members. Ann appreciated her accountability partner, as they were very experienced in their profession, yet treated Ann as an equal, and encouraged her to hold them accountable as well. The sessions created good feedback, coaching, and lessons for each member that had an accountability partner. Ann saw herself develop and provide feedback and accountability to her partner, even though Ann thought of her like a superior. The organization even showcased the session as a benefit on their website for potential members.

Meeting with the North Chamber of Commerce:

When Ann first scheduled to meet with the North Chamber of Commerce, it was shortly after she signed up and scheduled her calendar around the meetings and events she committed to with Our Empowering Women. She was enthused, as well as nervous, as the reality of the situation of commitments she was making weighed heavily on her mind. She, at times, would have doubt which brought the nervousness. But she then would have thoughts of determination and perseverance. She knew, that to make a change in her life, took a commitment. She was committed to seeing it through, and she would refocus herself on a vision of the end in mind. She could see herself successful and providing for her family with additional opportunities.

Ann arrived at the office of the North Chamber of Commerce to meet with a person named Monica. She informed the receptionist in the lobby that she was there to meet with Monica, whose title was Program Director. She sat down and waited a few minutes for Monica to arrive. While waiting, she noticed a newsletter on a coffee table next to her chair that she began reading from. It caught her eye as it was a newsletter on the North Chamber. What captured her interest most was an article titled, "Making A Difference" which showed several individuals wearing hard hats working on the frame of a house. The article spoke about Habitat For Humanity, and how the North Chamber of Commerce was contributing financially, as well as by providing volunteers. The article went in depth describing the need for low-income housing and the fight against poverty. The article explained how the North Chamber of Commerce community involvement initiative within its membership contributes to give back and how this is an important issue with the Chamber organization. Ann really appreciated the insight that the article gave as it made a very strong impression of the Chambers interactions and belief system. Ann remembered that another Chamber of Commerce within her review listed their values that included Community Involvement and Corporate Responsibility. But she had become concerned as through their website and with speaking with members, Ann found that this was not evident in their actions. So to see this demonstrated in action with the North Chamber of Commerce was reassuring and validated their commitment to their values system. Ann's nervousness subsided with this reassurance and it gave her a sense of comfort. At this moment, Monica appeared in the lobby.

"Ann?" Monica asked, while walking over to Ann.

Ann stood up from her chair to shake hands with Monica. "Yes, hello, I am Ann. Thank you for taking the time to meet with me."

Monica replied, "Ann, I am very excited to meet you. The organization you work for has been a member for years. We always appreciate their involvement. We regularly welcome new members, especially when they come from an expansion of existing memberships. Growth always allows us to expand and provide more."

"Thanks," Ann smiled.

It was at this moment that Monica gestured to a conference room that was visible from the lobby. "We can go in there and let's talk about your interest, as well as your goals."

"Okay," Ann responded, as she followed Monica to the conference room.

"Please have a seat," Monica stated, while gesturing to a chair. "I see you have been reading our newsletter. Is there something in particular that caught your interest?"

Ann replied, "I just started on the first article about your participation with Habitat For Humanity. It appears that involvement was an awesome way to give back."

"Oh, it was!" Monica replied, with excitement. "One of the many things I value here is our community involvement. I like that we put our values in action and that they are not just fancy words that may look good on paper. They really mean something to this organization and we live it."

"That is my belief as well," Ann answered. "Many organizations may want to create a good impression, so they build fancy

Mission, Vision, and Value Statements. However, when you meet their employees, they are unfamiliar with what those statements are or what they mean."

"Exactly," stated Monica, emphatically. "One of the biggest things I value here is we always speak about our Mission, Vision, and Values. We discuss them when we execute strategic planning. We ensure every committee we create understands each statement and that any decision they make must encompass the Mission, Vision, and Values of the organization. I have seen how important this is."

"I agree," Ann commented. "Our organization is very big in teaching this, and this is one of the reasons I enjoy working there. Our mission defines our purpose and why we exist. Our values define how we live each day. It is very important."

Monica started speaking, "We both can see and appreciate why it is important to us in the places that we work. But from our perspective at the chamber we believe it is a commitment to our members and the community we serve."

"I agree, as most organizations may not understand the importance. I appreciate that the chamber believes and demonstrates this," Ann approved.

"We need to demonstrate this, because as we build programs to benefit our members this one has to be foundational in our workshops. We have workshops on Mission, Vision, and Values that flow into our Strategic Planning workshops. We demonstrate how everything interlinks," Monica continued.

Ann started speaking, "This makes me appreciate and realize how fortunate I am within my employment. I have friends that complain about the places that they work, and how they believe they are under-appreciated. The sad part is they have a common belief that all jobs are this way. Perhaps most are, but they all think I am lucky too."

"Yes, it is nice to realize that your employer cares, and builds an environment for success," Monica empathized. "This is what we teach and try to provide to our members. Other members contribute and you will appreciate that the organization, along with its members, are all striving to be this type of organization. So we share and teach each other. Some organizations are mature in their culture and what they have built, while others want to continue to learn and develop. We strive to provide the education to fill that knowledge and skill gap."

This information and conversation excited Ann. It gave her affirmation that the North Chamber of Commerce would be a good choice for her to build a foundation of support. She was ready to proceed in the discussion with Monica, but unlike the Our Empowering Women Foundation, Ann was not sent any paperwork or questionnaires to fill out before the meeting with Monica.

"Ann," Monica spoke up, "your employer is a member here, so we have their information on file. But our process is more like an interview to discover more about you and what are your goals and aspirations. So let's start, and please ask if you need any clarity on my questions."

"Sounds good," Ann replied.

The interview began. "Ann, tell me about your professional background, your role, where you started, what you have learned, and how you have seen yourself change?" Monica asked.

Ann's answer was very thorough to allow Monica to understand her background. "My professional background has really taken strides forward since I have been with my current organization. I have worked as a teller in a bank and held other jobs like housekeeping. But I have always had the knack for understanding computer programs, as well as having the logic on how to utilize them efficiently."

"How long have you worked at your current organization?" Monica inquired.

"I have been there a little over a year," Ann replied. "I originally applied and started as an Administrative Assistant for the sales team. I would support the team, provide information and reports, and assist in meetings."

"Okay, tell me about your growth and advancement, and then we will get into your goals and objectives," Monica requested.

Ann started explaining, "Well, in a short time, my immediate supervisor and manager of the sales team, promoted me as his Executive Admin. He further worked on my training and development, and he encouraged me to expand on my ideas. As I learned the systems, like their Learning Management System, and their Customer Relations Management System known as CRM, I was able to logically figure out new reports and tracking that I was able to build. This gained attention from other departments, which was a surprise to me, but I was asked to fine-tune them for different needs. I was even sent to some additional training in both systems."

"That is awesome," Monica complimented. "Where did this take you next?"

"I would be asked to take on more responsibility, and even lead meetings," Ann continued. "Next, and up until now, I have been being mentored by our Vice President. I've been humbled by having my work so recognized. It was intimidating at first, but the Vice President has really been down to earth and has helped me lay out goals, objections, and the foundation of my personal mission, vision, and values."

"Wow, sounds like a great mentor," Monica praised. "Take me through the creation of your personal mission, vision, and values."

"Sure," Ann stated. "Let me grab what we created." Ann picked up her folder and grabbed a copy of her mission, vision, and values worksheet to hand to Monica. She handed Monica a copy and kept one out for herself.

Monica accepted the document and reviewed it. "This is awesome!" Monica admired. "I like how you lined out your principle statements, mission statement, and vision statement. Tell me about the highlighted letters that start each principle statement. It looks like they spell respect."

"They do spell respect," Ann affirmed. "The process was to first define my personal values. As our Vice President taught, my values are the foundation of everything I will do, and all decisions should point towards my values. It is from the values that I built my principle statements. I learned, and now understand, that values become principles when they become automatic. So the principle statements are my values in action. I ensured that with each one, I could make a commitment to live by them each day. The way we built them is by creating a monument word that if we remember the word, we will remember each principle statement. This is how we defined the word respect and built the statements to align in this manner."

> *The monument word allows you to memorize your principle statements because they are important to you.*

Monica then spoke, "I really like the process. The monument word allows you to memorize your principle statements because they are important to you. The statements really demonstrate your values in action, which allow others to comprehend what you stand for."

"Exactly," Ann stated. "This allowed me to learn and understand how successful organizations build upon the same process. They build a foundation first that consists of their values and principles, and as I was taught, this is what you will live by. This means what you will live by each day, and allows them to guide your direction. Every decision and plan should point back to your values and principles. This builds the foundation that your mission and vision statement will rest upon."

Monica was impressed and could see that Ann was sharp and well-spoken in explaining this process. "Ann, can you please tell me about building your mission statement and your vision statement?" Monica questioned further.

"Sure," Ann began. "As I was educated, your mission statement is external, and it defines your reason for existence. So deep down, why do you exist and how can you explain it to others. Also, by defining your mission statement and sharing it tells others what you want to be held accountable to. It is your commitment to yourself and to others. You can see that my mission statement is: To seek solutions and betterment of myself and others through compassion and effort, and to face the future with an optimistic outlook. So this is why I exist. With my values and principles providing the foundation, my mission leads me to where I need to go, and what I need to do to accomplish my mission. My mission should also provide value to others as well. I should be able to demonstrate how this benefits those I come in contact with."

Monica was excited by what she was hearing. "I certainly see the value and how you own and believe your mission statement. How is a vision statement different?"

"Okay," Ann responded. "As I stated, that a mission statement is external, a vision statement is internal meaning it is not public-facing. A vision statement defines where I want to be, and what I want to accomplish in the next 3 to 5 years, but with a Big Hairy Audacious Goal known as a BHAG. This is why it is internal. A vision statement, like mine, should be pulling from the front, and your mission statement pushes. It may be audacious in the goal or goals, but this allows you to evaluate and assess progress and milestone achievements."

Monica responded, "I understand. I like your vision statement. Within 3-years, to obtain financial independence earning an annual income of $65,000 or greater, and purchasing a 3-bedroom home, while having the ability to save 10% or more from income. To earn two promotions obtaining the role of Group Manager with my current employer, and utilize my skills, expertise, and blessings to donate one day per week working with abused women. Finally, paying it forward by mentoring two women at a time, that aspire to become leaders and advance. I see it is expansive and has several challenges. But I also see how a solid foundation of values and principles, and a firm mission statement as a guide, lead to a vision that can be accomplished."

"This is why each adds a piece to the process of building," Ann stated. "With these in place, they guide everything and they allow you to build your goals, objectives, development plan, and accountability plan. You can see why some organizations have a strong culture built from this foundation, and why others suffer."

"I certainly can," Monica replied. "Obviously we have programs that work with our organizations and individual members on how to build these. I believe your participation will add value. Ann, lets next talk about your goals and objectives, and how you see how this chamber enhancing them."

"Sure," Ann answered. "This whole process I learned from our Vice President. We walked through starting with me executing a self-assessment on my leadership traits and skills, and then having my peers and superiors assess me as well. It was humbling and made me nervous. But the assessments helped level set me for the process of setting goals and objectives and then fine-tuning those for what I need from a support system. This is why I am here, to build a support system."

"Explain what you mean by a support system?" Monica inquired.

"Sure," Ann stated. "Because my goals would create new heights and have an impact on my personal life as well as my professional life, it is important for me to have a support system outside of my family, friends, and current environment. My goals and objectives will take a commitment and create a change in habits and actions that will require support from those that may have done and achieved something similar. Also, it will be important to have encouragers, advisors, and mentors. Our Vice President teaches, that the more expanded the support system, the quicker one will regain confidence when adversity hits, and they will move forward. Certainly having a support system with family is important. However, they may also be some of the first distractors and naysayers because some of the commitments may alter their lifestyle with me directly. This is why an expanded network is essential."

Monica appreciated the answer. "I would agree with your answer. My belief is the same, but it was important to understand what you mean as a support system. I would agree, as I have seen others who believed they had a good family support system get sidetracked because their commitment alters home life and then family regrets and resists the change."

"Yes," Ann commented. "Although I am optimistic of my support from home, I could foresee receiving some push back."

"Thanks, Ann," Monica replied. "So, let's go over your goals and objectives. Now when I ask about goals and objectives, I am not asking for you to list them out for me. What I would like to have you speak to is an overview of what you would like to accomplish and achieve? Where do you want to excel, and see yourself in a few years? Tell me your story."

"Certainly," Ann began. "The process I went through was to define my personal goals and then my professional goals. This was helpful as I can see that they overlap. From each, I was able to define objectives for achievement and development."

"That sounds like a solid process," Monica replied. "Please proceed."

Ann proceeded, "My personal goals are built around owning a home in three years. Gaining financial independence with the ability to save 10-percent of my income, also in that time frame. I have a 401k savings goal with a 20-year outreach. So you can see, to achieve this, it would have to be tied to the success of professional goals and development."

Monica spoke, "They are strong goals, and yes, definitely would be tied to achieving professional success."

"Yes," Ann answered. "I have additional personal goals for my son, as well as for helping abused women. These are of great value to me. But for my professional goals I would like to develop into leadership within my current organization. I would like to earn two promotions over the next 3 to 5 years and help develop others. This would definitely require my growth in skills and knowledge."

"What skills and knowledge have you identified that would assist your development and advancement?" Monica inquired.

Ann responded with her overview. "I need to learn more about financial management, as this helps me both personally and professionally. There are processes I need to learn that structure a good process from good habits. But to expand on skills, I listed things like emotional intelligence, which allows me to understand and manage individuals effectively. Communication skills, persuasion, assertiveness, resilience, listening, decision-making, and strategic thinking are all to expand on."

"That is a solid list," mused Monica. "How do you foresee this organization assisting you?"

"I made two lists," Ann replied. "One list is what I defined as the pros and cons of the organization. In the second list I defined what my needs are. This allowed me to make my choices."

"What are those choices?" Monica asked.

Ann looked at another page that she had. "Number 1, I need an accountability partner. This is someone that I meet with once a month and who holds me accountable. Ideally I can provide the same. Number two is that I need to find a mentor or two. Number three, is that I need emotional support. This would come as I develop relationships through trust. Number 4, I would need the insight of others. Now this will come from mentors, but from other individuals who have become successful and those who are growing in their success. Number 5, stability, as well as consistency, as this comes from good programs with solid attendees. Number 6, is to be challenged. This means I need to be challenged when we do projects, assignments, and have goals and objectives. I believe we all need others to help push us."

Monica held her hand up for Ann to pause for a moment. "Let me catch up, as I am writing these down for your file, as well as for my reference to teach others." Monica wrote for a minute and then signaled she was ready.

Ann continued. "I believe I was on number 7. Number 7 is camaraderie, which is important, or I would lose interest or lack effort. No matter how a person may be committed, camaraderie helps drive interest and commitment. Number 8, is to have access to experience. To be around individuals who have experience in developing others, experience in building a business, and running a team is invaluable. Experience also from those that have had failures and overcame them. This is why this organization excites me."

"We definitely have members filled with experience," Monica replied. "What I value most is their openness to share with others."

"Yes, I agree," stated Ann, confidently. "The final three are, number 9, to have access to different levels of knowledge. This means there are those that have small business experience, as well as those all the way up to large corporate America. In addition, someone who may be a one-person self-employed business has a different experience than others. Number 10, is to have access to different skill levels. Which is similar to different levels of experience, but focused on skills."

"You definitely did your work," Monica marveled. "This is a great list and I believe we can be a good match for these."

Ann spoke up, "Yes, but you don't have to be a match for each one. You might be, but I have chosen another resource too, along with my mentorship from our Vice President. So even if we have overlap in some areas that would be okay."

Ann and Monica carried on the conversation some more. Ann explained to Monica about Our Empowering Women, and what she wants to sign up with there. Monica reviewed the networking schedule, and which one she believed would add value to Ann. Monica then reviewed some workshops on the schedule and their objectives. These had a couple within the alignment of Ann's objectives. Monica explained about the orientation that she would like Ann to attend, and also spoke about wanting to introduce Ann to a member or two, perhaps over a scheduled lunch. Ann agreed. The discussion carried forward and Ann achieved her purpose in outlining a schedule to start with that did not overwhelm her.

Monica thanked Ann, "I really appreciate our meeting. Can I keep your list of values and principles, with your mission and vision? I would like to show this to others."

"Certainly," replied Ann, as she walked to the door. "I truly am excited, but if you ever see I need a push, you have my permission."

Ann's Principle Statements

Respect yourself first and demonstrate respect for others.

Earn trust daily and reward others that do the same.

Seek fun in all you do and let others enjoy and celebrate success.

Passion is the objective, results are the achievement.

Execute with initiative and seek innovation.

Count accountability as your responsibility to yourself and others.

Taste the hunger for what feeds you and drives you to the next level.

Ann's Mission Statement:

To seek solutions and betterment of myself and others through compassion and effort, and to face the future with an optimistic outlook.

Ann's Vision Statement:

Within 3-years, to obtain financial independence earning an annual income of $65,000 or greater, and purchasing a 3-bedroom home while having the ability to save 10% or more from income. To earn two promotions obtaining the role of Group Manager with my current employer, and utilize my skills, expertise and blessings to donate one day per week working with abused women. Finally, paying it forward by mentoring two women at a time, that aspire to become leaders and advance.

End

Ann's sync up with her Vice President:

Ann and I synced up after her meetings with Our Empowering Women and the North Chamber of Commerce. I believed it was important to gain insight from Ann if her choices for a support system aligned with what she had determined they needed to provide. Also, it was important to step back, level set which ones would provide for which areas of need, and at what time. I learned from experience that someone like Ann, who is determined and excited to be taking these steps, may have moments that over-enthusiasm could drive her into making commitments that become too hard to follow through on. We all believe we can accomplish a lot, which is good. But a good mentor will ensure that we do not over commit ourselves in our scheduling and knowledge gain commitments.

Ann and I reviewed the Development Plan we had outlined earlier as we spoke about Ann's meetings with each organization. Ann was excited to share the details on each. What Ann also realized is that there would be overlap on what each could provide. She believed that within each organization she would define a mentor or two. She also hoped that as she grew she would find those she could mentor and be a part of their support network. She had a better understanding of how the interaction would help her grow. Mentoring others would be a big confidence booster. Many women who aspire to be leaders may not view themselves as highly as others see them, so this is important. Humility is important, but confidence is important too. To have a belief in yourself is a foundation needed for growth, as it allows one to develop a larger belief that they can progress more.

Ann listed on a whiteboard what she would like to sign up for in each organization, Our Empowering Women and the North Chamber of Commerce. I asked Ann questions and also discussed some of the items that could be accomplished on the job. As per the Development Plan that we lined out, I reminded Ann that our organization had access to Ann attending Dale Carnegie Leadership Certification, which I was committed to providing. There were also the book reading and reviews that I would mentor Ann on that included the 7 Habits of Highly Effective People, The Rockefeller Habits, The One Minute Manager, and 5 Dysfunctions of a Team. Ann was thankful for my commitment and mentorship. However, she listed many things, which is common for aspiring women leaders as they have a strong belief they can accomplish a lot. I cautioned and helped her to prioritize the list so as to trim it down a little. We agreed that we would review the list at least once every six months so that it would allow us to add more or slow the pace as needed. The important part was to define solid SMART Goals and to measure that knowledge gain was occurring.

After about an hour at the meeting following Ann's visit to the North Chamber of Commerce, Ann believed she had a good starting point. She had the outline of a Development Plan with all the information from her choices and objectives from Our Empowering Women, North Chamber of Commerce, and her mentorship that I committed to. I encouraged Ann to review the plan with direct family members, whom she believed she already had support and commitment from. I instructed her that it was important to keep them in the loop, especially at the beginning, as well as at certain intervals throughout the process. I also requested she take a few days and flesh her plan out more and when complete to provide me an electronic copy, which would allow me to support, follow, and help with accountability. Working with others, I have found it helpful to demonstrate my awareness of timelines, to ask questions, show encouragement, and mentor. Ann followed the recommendations and met with her family. She did receive a little hesitation from her husband and from her son, which surprised her. However, the hesitation or concerns were due to how much she was committing to and how that would affect the normal routines around the house, which added commitments from them too. This is an aspect not always thought of earlier. However, they all agreed to support the plan and support Ann in her next steps.

Development Action Plan

Employee Name: **Date:**

Job Role: **Manager:**

Action Item:

Specifics	Owner:	Measure:	Due Date:	Comments

Not Started   In Process   Complete

Ann puts her support network plan into action:

Ann had her plan complete and updated. She and I met, for a quick review and to provide an electronic copy. I created a file on a shared drive in the organization's LMS and demonstrated to Ann how we both could access it. I recommended that Ann schedule a specific time each week that she would ensure it was updated. We agreed this would be on Mondays, prior to 4 p.m. This will allow me, to know it was updated, should I wish to review it.

Soon, a month had passed. Ann had started the process of attending meetings, attending a college class, and working on reading one of the books listed in her Development Plan. It was an added load, which at first, she could feel the pressure of managing a work life and a home life together with new commitments. But she was accomplishing the plan day by day. She received mentoring from me, as we would meet to discuss the book assignment, which also allotted for additional mentoring time. She also was establishing relationships with individuals at the North Chamber of Commerce and Our Empowering Women. She, at times, would feel overwhelmed. After discussing this with a mentor at Our Empowering Women, Ann could see how this individual had similar feelings, especially early in her development. This mentor would tell her about the situations she had encountered and how she would take steps one day at a time. She would coach Ann on some stress-relieving techniques and really pushed the mindset that pressures will come and it is best to learn how to face them rather than to let them cause too much stress that can cause disruptions and even illness. This coaching and mentoring received was valuable to Ann.

One day, about six weeks into the start of Ann's plan, I noticed Ann was quiet. Sometimes it is not too difficult to pick up from one's actions and demeanor that something is not right. It was evident that something was bothering Ann. When I had a moment of available time, I asked Ann to come to my office. Not knowing what the issue might be, I believed privacy was the best option which would also allow for the discussion to be more open and revealing. At least as open as Ann would allow. Ann arrived and entered my office.

"Hello, Ann," I greeted her. "Please go ahead and close the door behind you."

"Okay," Ann stated, as she walked over to the chair by my desk and sat down.

"How are things today?" I asked.

"They are okay," Ann spoke slowly.

"Ann, it seems that you are preoccupied, or that something is bothering you," I began. "Is there something I can assist you with or that you would like to talk about?"

Ann seemed a little hesitant and it appeared she wiped a tear from her eye. "Just some pressures from home," she answered. She continued to look down and away.

"I understand if it is a private situation, Ann," I replied. "Just let me know. But if I could tell something was bothering you, others will see it too. As a mentor, I welcome the opportunity to listen, as well as provide insight if you wish."

Ann remained quiet for a moment before she started to speak. "It is just pressures that are occurring at home. Something I do not need. My husband is starting to question me attending my meetings and other things I have committed to in my development plan that take away my attention from him or from home. He questioned if it was a waste of time and made me feel that I was incapable."

I listened, and was not surprised, as I have seen circumstances like this many times. Especially with an aspiring woman leader who is taking their first steps towards working on their development. The process is a commitment and it alters home life. One has to believe that the sacrifices of the present will pay dividends and rewards for the future. But human nature is that spouses may commit and say they will support the changes when discussed, but once they realize and start experiencing what the changes and commitments mean, they then may question and push back. Unfortunately, some men are insecure and short-sighted. This is usually one of the first and common situations that arise. Many aspiring women relent and give up their dream to keep the peace. Ann would need to assess the dream, her home life, as well as her husband. This must be a two-way assessment, not a one-way.

"Ann," I started, "This is one of the reasons we build a support network that is more than just your immediate family. Also, as you remember, this is why we also pushed for you to have several discussions with family because it is important they know the details and what the commitment really means. Did your husband not understand what the commitment would mean? Also, is there something that has changed on his side?"

Ann hesitated before answering. "I believe I was clear in laying everything out. That is what is frustrating me now. Although, he says he did not realize that it would take me away as much as it has. But what hurts most is his reference to whether I am capable of completing the process and advancing my career."

I observed, as Ann's speech demonstrated that she was hurt and bothered by the situation. "Ann, I know that things can be hurtful when spoken from those close to us, especially a spouse. However, I must state that this is common, and I have seen it many times as someone like you aspires to grow. To grow, it takes commitment to learn and develop. This change alters every aspect of your life."

"But he knew all of this beforehand," Ann blurted out. "I followed your instructions and informed him of the whole process. I walked him through my options and even asked for his insight and opinions. I did this and he said he supported it."

"I know, I know," I repeated myself. "Once again, this is very common. Unfortunately, some spouses will even use tactics that demean and hurt in an attempt to push the spouse into dropping out."

"He did that!" Ann interrupted. "He reminded me that I first applied as an admin role and insinuated that was my capabilities. It was hurtful what he stated as he questioned that if I fail, it would be a big waste of time."

"Did you ask and remind him of what this does when you succeed?" I asked. "This will not be the first time this discussion will arise. However, this is exactly why we had you build a support network. I am here to support and provide advice as a mentor and from one who has mentored others to success. I hesitate to get too involved in your direct marriage situation. But I will say that you are very capable and I believe you will grow and succeed. I would not desire to waste my time with someone who would not. My time and energy are important to me, as are the individuals I invest time in as well. By choosing to mentor and work with you, defines that I have already assessed that you have all the capabilities needed for success."

"I did mention what the rewards are as I grow, develop, and succeed," she replied. "This is when he seemed more focused on possible failure than success."

I paused for a moment, as these discussions are delicate. "Here is what I suggest. As I stated, this is exactly why we had you build a support network, and it is at times like these that I recommend you seek answers from your mentors. I know you have a few women mentors that have built success. It is one, or a couple, of these that I recommend you seek counsel, as each can give guidance and share their experiences."

Ann paused as a sign of hesitation or concern. "This is a little embarrassing, to discuss push back from home."

My response was quick, "I believe they will surprise you with their response, counsel, and support. Also, if they are true mentors, they will allow you to show vulnerability. You will do the same when you pay it forward in the future. If you believe you have chosen the right mentors, then this will be demonstrated by their actions. Finally, because they have built and developed themselves to become successful, they will understand your challenge, as I guarantee you they encountered challenges in their journey too. Their experience is what will help you."

Ann listened and agreed. Her demeanor had changed to be at peace with the next steps and determined to stay on the path she had chosen. "I will reach out to a couple now and see when we can speak or meet."

"That is a great idea," I stated. Ann stood up from the chair and I walked her to the office door. "Let me know how it goes and if there is anything I can assist with," I told her, as she was exiting.

"Thanks," Ann replied. She walked out and towards the next office space where her work area was.

Ann left the office feeling better about the situation and more determined to work through the issue. She remembered being warned about obstacles and setbacks by me long before setting anything in motion. She now understood why I was adamant in establishing a support network that expanded past her immediate family. She remembered how she even pushed back a little because she believed strongly that she had the support of her immediate family, and believed lack of support would not come from this area. She was glad that I insisted, as she realized she could trust in my judgment and experience. Ann placed a call to two separate mentors she spoke with, both of whom were with Our Empowering Women. She also had a mentor with the North Chamber of Commerce, but wanted to start with these two, as one had a family with a child, and had built her success while being a wife and mother. The other, Kendra, is a single mother, and Ann did not know too much about the specifics of her home life history, but admired this mentor for being well-grounded in the right values. Ann received a call back from Sally, the married mentor, and they were able to schedule lunch. Soon after she received a call back from Kendra, the single mother, and they agreed to have a phone conversation in the early evening.

Ann's counsel with her mentor Sally:

Ann met Sally at a local sit-down restaurant. She thanked Sally for making herself available. "Thank you for meeting with me, I truly appreciate it."

Sally looked baffled by the comment. "No problem! I told you to never hesitate to reach out. You and I agreed that I would be one of your mentors. I would not have agreed if I would not have been so committed."

Sally and Ann placed their food orders and with simple conversation transitioned into Ann's situation by the time the food arrived. "I wanted to speak with you and gain some insight and advice. With my pursuing my goals and working on personal development, my husband is starting to push back on the commitments I have made and how it affects our home life. Before attending meetings and programs, I would be at home each evening with our son. With the commitments, which we spoke about before I committed to the meetings and programs, he is having to alter what he does and now that he sees how that affects him, he seems to want me to drop out of my commitment and let everything go back to how it was."

Sally listened intently. It was a familiar story. Not just from what she heard from others she had mentored, but also what she experienced personally. "Ann," Sally began. "I know you have told me the details before, but I will ask again, okay?"

"Okay," Ann responded.

Sally continued, "Before you made the decision that you wanted to grow and develop and advance yourself professionally, did you have this discussion with your husband and what was his response?"

"Yes," Ann responded. "We spoke of it several times, as well as in many different ways. Several times I would describe my aspirations and how I wanted to develop, and my husband would respond with support and encouragement. He would even reply with comments like, 'You should look into that.' So it is with his encouragement that the hunger to move forward grew."

"Okay," Sally commented. "What were some of the other ways?"

Ann answered, "We would talk about dreams and goals. At present we live paycheck to paycheck and we rent, as we have never owned a home of our own. So in conversations, we would talk about what it would take to get ahead. This would always circle back to how I could advance and provide more, and we would also speak on areas he could grow and contribute. We would encourage and support each other. This is why the push back hurts and is a surprise."

Sally spoke up, "Marriage is not always easy, as it is something both sides have to work on. Marriage has a roadblock called humans and humans have emotions. Sometimes those emotions are driven by fear of change and what else that change can bring. Other times it is ego. As one partner in the marriage starts doing better the other side may have their ego bruised. This is where you need to make some determinations."

"Determinations?" Ann asked. "What do you mean by determinations?"

"Let me take a step back and describe a similar situation I went through," Sally replied.

"Okay," Ann nodded in agreement.

"What you are describing, I went through as well," Sally went on. "In fact, scenarios like this are common from others I have mentored. Let me describe mine, and perhaps this will help."

"Okay," Ann responded, eagerly.

"Like you, I started at an admin level, but flourished in the role," Sally began. "Soon, I was recognized and being mentored for the next stages of development. I was viewed as a person who had leadership skills that, with development and investment, could grow within the organization. I communicated my desires and goals with my husband and he stated he would be supportive. We spoke about how it would alter home life, especially with a young daughter, and he agreed that the decision was worth what little sacrifice it was at the moment. I believed everything was set and I started implementing my development plan, which altered my schedule and took me away from home a few hours per week. It was with this reality that my husband started to push back. Sometimes it was brought about by something happening to him that day. There are so many factors that one cannot think of beforehand that can occur that affects the daily life from both sides. One time his work needed him to stay later, but I already had a program to attend. So at first, the arguments were about whose job was more important. Next, the argument was about if the sacrifice was even worth the potential payoff, or was it a pipe dream. One thing I did know is that I valued my marriage and family, so the issue had to be addressed."

"So what happened?" Ann asked. "I know you are still married."

"Yes," Sally replied. "This was about 16-years ago and we stayed married. To us, that was not the issue. However, we did have to have some hard and honest discussions. I needed to allow him to explain his feelings and he needed to allow me the same. I know of some others that even attended counseling and worked through it. The most important thing is they agreed to have the discussion and set boundaries."

"Boundaries? What do you mean by boundaries?" Ann inquired.

"I asked my husband for us to have a discussion on the situation, but that we needed to set rules so that it would not escalate," Sally explained. "The rules would allow him the opportunity to speak and me the equal opportunity. We agreed to be vulnerable with each other, as sometimes this gets lost in marriages. But it was important to discuss and understand each other's feelings and concerns."

"How did the conversation go?" Ann asked.

Sally spoke up with a smile, "It was the foundation on how we have difficult discussions today. It allowed us to first realize that our love and our marriage is important. So the ground rules were set into place with respect for our marriage as the first priority. He was able to discuss his frustration, and even some insecurities with me advancing and developing. He was honest about how things made him feel and it allowed me to reassure him, but also understand how I may have been triggering those insecurities."

"And when it was your turn?" Ann pressed.

"It was reassuring in both ways," Sally responded. "I expressed the importance of our marriage, but also the importance of my growth and advancement. We spoke about the fact that everything I was doing I had received his support from the start, and how I appreciated and admired him for that. I expressed how his commitment and support was an emotional high, and his recent push back was an emotional low. Finally, I expressed the importance of me staying the course, and us having routine discussions on where things stand and how we can support each other. He agreed and stated that he did not want to renege, but if we see it causing problems that we needed to address them. We spoke about other resources, like my mom who lives close by, or a neighborhood babysitter in case one of us runs late. We became more proactive about solutions instead of waiting for things to occur."

"This sounds encouraging," Ann replied. "I hope my husband and I can have a similar discussion. Did things get easier from there?"

"Depends on which things you are asking about?" Sally responded. "As far as challenges, those still occurred, but we had more ways to address them. My husband and I had a problem-solving process. As far as commitments, I must be honest and state that those grew and hit a more challenging stage. They will for you too, as it is like climbing a mountain to get to the other side. This is an important aspect, to be honest, that more challenges will come because the dream and payoff are beneficial and rewarding. This would not come without challenges. So make sure you do not deceive each other in thinking that challenges will diminish, but be honest that although they may increase,

> *More challenges will come because the dream and payoff are beneficial and rewarding.*

that you will both be committed to working through them."

Ann appreciated Sally sharing her story and even stated as such. "Sally, I really appreciate you sharing your story, as this gives me some insight."

Sally responded, "This is what being a mentor means, to be vulnerable. Much of our mentoring is what we have experienced ourselves, or education by our mentors. This is why paying it forward is so important. My biggest question to you is, are you committed to your goals?"

Ann responded quickly, "Yes, this is something I truly want to accomplish. It would be so rewarding and satisfying."

"Then understand that there will be barriers," Sally stated, sincerely. "But be committed to addressing them head-on. Much like you will with this one."

Sally further explained how her husband became her biggest supporter. He watched her advance and was happy for her. Over the next 16-years their marriage and professional careers each took different turns, but their support for each other flourished through many ups and downs. Sally and Ann finished lunch and walked out of the restaurant. Ann returned to the office enthused, yet a little nervous as she knew she had to confront and address the situation.

Ann meets with her mentor, Kendra:

Ann worked throughout the day, thinking about her situation and the advice that Sally gave her. She knew that she would need to address the situation with her husband. She hoped and believed he would be willing to have an open discussion. She valued her marriage and believed he did too. Differences happen in relationships, and those built on love and trust will work through the issues and strengthen the marriage. Ann and Kendra agreed to a phone conversation after work hours at 5:30 p.m. She looks forward to hearing Kendra's perspective. Kendra was a fireball of a businesswoman, well respected, and very focused. She was a good accountability partner for Ann, keeping her on task, and providing good advice. Soon it was time for Ann to call Kendra.

Ann selected Kendra's number on her cell phone and called. "Hi Kendra," Ann greeted, as soon as Kendra answered.

"Hello, Ann, how are you?" Kendra asked. "I have been looking forward to speaking with you today."

"Thanks," Ann replied. "Me as well. I appreciate you being there for me, as a friend, as well as a mentor."

"This is what mentors do," Kendra told her. "We listen, offer advice, and hold accountable. As a friend, I will be here as well. So, let's dive in. Tell me what can I help with?"

Ann went into the same explanation she had given to Sally, with the same details. She explained her feelings of sabotage and hurt, as she had believed her husband had committed to supporting her decision and the changes that would come from it. Kendra asked for clarification in a few areas and asked Ann how the situation was making her feel. She also asked how Ann's husband felt. This was an interesting question and Ann had to give it some thought. Kendra suggested that this would be a good question for Ann to ask her husband and to gain an understanding of his feelings and what was driving them. Ann appreciated the advice.

Kendra listened and provided solid feedback. Then Kendra inserted into the conversation that her story was similar, in regards to the push back and withdrawal of support from her husband when she launched into her development plan to advance in knowledge and skills. But it was important to Kendra to explain a few more details.

"Ann, as I mentioned, I received similar push back from my husband back when I set out in my development plan," Kendra began. "But it is important that if you know my story, that you are aware of the finer details. This was around 11-years ago that things transpired. Our son was around 3-years old. I was succeeding in my role within my employment and aspired to develop and become a leader and entrepreneur. I was presented with an opportunity to advance and my husband said he would fully support it. However, when he started to notice changes and what it meant for our home life routines is when he started to push back."

"Sounds like this is very common," Ann stated. "So what happened next, and what will you recommend?"

Kendra spoke, "Yes, this is very common. I have witnessed others receive push back from their children to their parents and siblings, who they believed would support and encourage them.

This is why this push back hurts. Because it is from those that we are close to. But this is why it is important that you surround yourself with others who have succeeded through the process."

"Yes, that was solid advice I received from my Vice President," Ann replied.

"He provided good advice," Kendra commented. "Anyway, it is important to understand that although this situation occurs often, the backgrounds may be different. As you know, I am single, so at some point I got divorced. But I would advise anyone to take one step at a time to have a discussion and work on the marriage. In my situation there were other factors before and after this situation that created a division in our marriage. I was in a marriage that, at times, my husband was demeaning to me. We worked on it, or so I believed we were trying to. But as he would refuse counseling and verbal abuse continued I had to make a decision for my happiness, and health for me and my son. Our environment was not healthy for him. He has a good relationship with his father, which is important."

"Thanks, Kendra," Ann replied. "Your openness is appreciated. It does scare me a little, as I do value my marriage."

"It is exactly for that reason that you must have a discussion with your husband," Kendra stated, firmly. "You owe it to your marriage, as well as to your son. A strong marriage is one where you share your concerns and your feelings. Not one where you hide them."

Ann nodded to herself in agreement. "I agree. I just need to move forward. I appreciate the discussion and insight.

"You are welcome," Kendra responded. "Let me know how it goes or if you need anything else."

"Thanks again," Ann said, warmly.

Ann and Kendra completed the call and disconnected. She gave thought to both conversations and realized that it was important to address and have the discussion with her husband. Her mentors gave her courage, along with their sound advice.

Ann addresses the situation:

Ann learned that confrontation is a benefit. This is just as important in business as it is within home life. Great leaders confront issues and learn how to navigate effectively with each one. If not addressed, one can create a scenario where they walk on eggshells, which destroys growth. Ann realized that because she valued her marriage, her husband's feelings, and the environment they created for raising their son, addressing the issue was important.

Ann and her husband agreed to have the discussion. They both explained they wanted the best for each other, and the change just created some stress and issues. Ann's husband listened to Ann on her dreams, and how the push back made her feel. She then asked her

* * * * * * * * * * *

Understanding how issues can cause each other to feel was powerful and allowed them to be more cognizant moving forward.

* * * * * * * * * * *

husband to discuss why the push back and his feelings. He opened up. The discussion was very therapeutic and the process became a precursor to how they would handle disagreements. Understanding how issues can cause each other to feel was powerful and allowed them to be more cognizant moving forward. Her husband agreed to stand behind her and support the decisions they had made. Moving forward, other issues would arise. Sometimes plans had to be changed or adjusted, but they learned to work through them. They found success in their marriage which provided peace of mind with Ann. She excelled and progressed through her plan.

At other times, Ann would have other issues she would need to address, and seek counsel on. I continued to be a mentor, and when issues would be addressed with me, I would push Ann through problem-solving routines to improve her skills. No matter how well a plan is written there will always be a roadblock or two, as there were with Ann's. When events or courses would get canceled, Ann would learn to simply work through the process and redefine the next steps. Ann developed other mentors as she grew and she began mentoring others. Some of the opportunities of mentoring others would just present themselves as others around her would view her as a successful individual driving to bigger heights.

Chapter 5

RIDE THE MOMENTUM

Ann was executing her development plan and enjoying the support that her network had brought her. She was learning new skills and knowledge that helped her advance while implementing each with confidence. It is funny how confidence builds more confidence, and soon it becomes infectious. Momentum is a positive influence, and one needs to learn how to ride the momentum for as long as possible. Certainly, Ann would encounter other hurdles and roadblocks, but her instincts were automatic in what it took to problem solve and work through each encounter. Ann developed a strong realm of mentors of differing skills, experience, and knowledge. She was also mentoring others which brought enjoyment, a sense of accomplishment, and a purpose for each day. Ann stayed consistent, and to protect what she was developing and building, she learned to ride the momentum and stay focused. She learned the power of consistent evaluation.

The Value of Evaluation:

Over some time, and through mentoring, I would educate Ann and demonstrate that at different intervals she would need to implement an evaluation process to assess success. She would do so at different intervals and with different experiences and encounters. I would always preach, and teach to the leadership team that with all plans the evaluation process is important. The purpose and importance of an evaluation process are always to test and assess how the plan is working, and what, if any, improvements or adjustments are warranted. An evaluation process is not looking for wholesale changes, but small improvements that bring good execution, or results, to great results. Also, this allows for additional learning that is shared with mentors as well as those we mentor. This is part of the process that keeps everyone learning, and momentum rolling. This is why mentorship is so valuable.

Ann was a year into her development and growth. However, she remembered early in the process, at the implementation stage, that she had asked how she could ensure improvement continues for success and long-term sustainability. She remembered the conversation and the education she received during several mentoring session we conducted.

"As I proceed with each plan, how does one ensure improvement moves in the right direction and continues with positive results?" Ann asked.

"That is a great question," I responded. "Think about many things you witness here in our business. Large or small, when we implement anything we always build in an evaluation process with a set timeline of execution."

"Yes, I believe I understand," Ann mused. "Much like the sales team execution plans that when we changed the plans, we assessed our progress at 90-days."

"Exactly," I replied. "If you remember, we already built an assessment form that allowed us to track details and dates, but also allowed feedback from those involved. We addressed concerns and we had measurements built-in that would allow us to see if progress was being made."

"Yes, I remember," Ann stated. "But we also added an item or two to the evaluation as things went forward."

"Correct," I agreed. "We build the model, but are open for anything that adds constructive value. By constructive value, I mean that it asks a good question, or brings forth a good measurement or view that allows insight. What it does not do, is try to sway the evaluation in one way or another. It remains objective and not subjective."

Ann understood, and within our sessions we built in an evaluation process and timeline with each. This also allowed her to work in our sessions, to build any additional assessments, working from the models that had been utilized in the past. Ann has shared this process with her mentors and also implements with those she mentors, as paying it forward is important. Her education has come full circle. Ann has seen the small adjustments that have paid dividends to success. She has also witnessed moments where she may have been tempted to make wholesale changes, but where the assessment showed progress and allowed her to decide to stay the course. This is natural, at times, as some plans may bring about changes that are uncomfortable, yet beneficial. Staying the course brings about big growth. When one goes outside their comfort zone is when they make leaps and bounds on development.

Many aspects within growth and development need measurement through evaluation systematically, and consistently. Time frames will differ based upon what is being evaluated and the time frame from which it was built. Several that Ann had built warranted evaluating on an annual basis. As other items with a longer focus would need evaluation within a 3 to 5 year timeframe.

Leadership Traits and Skills 360: (Annually)

Early in the process, as shown in Chapter One, Ann and I worked through an assessment of her Leadership Traits through her own self-assessment as well as by reaching out to her peers, and a few superiors, to provide feedback and recommendations by those involved. As stated in Chapter One, each trait listed three possible categories, 1. Needs Improvement, 2. Meets Standards, 3. Exceeds. Between each trait, we created a space for any comments, as comments were both welcomed and sought after. As instructed by me, Ann self-evaluated herself and wrote in her comments and feedback. We asked the others to execute the same in regards to Ann and send them in anonymously. The first time I worked with Ann on the evaluation process, we set a schedule for her to execute it again at the one year mark, and continue annually.

"Ann, as I stated when we first executed the Leadership Traits Evaluation, you must re-evaluate at certain intervals that allow you to measure progress, make adjustments, and utilize the results for your development plans," I stated.

Ann replied, "Yes, I do remember. But I also know that in any plan we create we need to always have an evaluation process so we can always be improving. Defining how that works may be different based upon the plan."

"Exactly," I responded. "Strategic plans, initiatives, and all other plans need to always have a timely assessment consisting of a re-evaluation, measurement, adjustments, and new execution plans."

"Okay, so with the leadership traits 360 do we just resend it to the original participants that we sent to the first time?" Ann questioned.

"We could do it that way," I answered. "But with your expansion with additional mentors, peers outside of business, and those you mentor, I would like to broaden the scope that includes several of these individuals with some that participated the first time. Let's make a list."

Ann and I started with revising the list of the original participants from her first assessment. One of the participants had left our organization and another had moved to a different department. From this point, I asked Ann to add her direct mentors, from which she added one from Our Empowering Women and one from the North Chamber of Commerce. She then started to name and add to the list a few additional peers she had developed relationships with in these groups. I recommended three to five, and she added four. Finally, we added two individuals she was mentoring, as their insight would add value, and their participation would introduce them to the process and provide additional education. This would allow them to learn through Ann's mentoring.

"Okay, so here is the list," Ann stated.

We reviewed the names and trimmed down the list by eliminating two repeats so the list would consist of equal repeat participants and new participants. We developed an email that would educate the new participants and define their execution with timelines. In addition, we discussed that we would ask the repeat participants to provide additional feedback defining areas they deemed Ann had demonstrated growth beyond expectations or needed more attention based upon their original assessment.

Mark Villareal
People, Strategy, Execution

Leadership Traits Evaluation

Please evaluate the leader listed based upon the following criteria:
1. Needs Improvement   2. Meets Standards   3. Exceeds Standards

In addition, please evaluate with high expectations of leadership. Please leave an explanation for any score of 1. Needs Improvement, for the individual being evaluated to gain insight for development.

Exceeds Standards should be rare, and must have a comment with an example on why you scored in that manner.

Trait   1. Needs Improvement   2. Meets Standards   3. Exceeds Standards

1 *Vision*　　☐　　　　☐　　　　☐
The leader shares the vision constantly, clearly, and points to small victories and progress.
Comment: _____

2 *Communication* ☐　　　☐　　　　☐
The leader must communicate constantly and effectively. Addressing important issues quickly.
Comment: _____

3 *Decisiveness*　☐　　　　☐　　　　☐
A leader must be decisive, yet with wisdom based upon sound facts. Decisions are made timely and with confidence.
Comment: _____

4 *Integrity/Honesty* ☐　　　☐　　　　☐
The leader demonstrates and has earned trust through integrity and shows transparency.
Comment: _____

5 *Inspiration*　☐　　　　☐　　　　☐
A leader must inspire and gain followers through belief in their leadership of others.
Comment: _____

6 *Optimism*　☐　　　　☐　　　　☐
Leaders must have the ability to instill optimism to those that follow as well as to peers and superiors.
Comment: _____

7 *Facilitation* ☐ ☐ ☐

The leader has a strong ability to lead and facilitate their team and others to focus on goal achievement.

Comment: _____

8 *Commitment* ☐ ☐ ☐

The leader demonstrates genuine commitment and passion that followers, peers, and superiors believe in.

Comment: _____

9 *Accountability* ☐ ☐ ☐

The leader accepts accountability and holds others accountable for high standards and achievement.

Comment: _____

10 *Empowerment* ☐ ☐ ☐

The leader defines parameters that empower and develops others to take action and make decisions.

Comment: _____

11 *Creativity* ☐ ☐ ☐

The leader has shown creativity and innovation for new ideas and embraces the same from their team.

Comment: _____

12 *Empathy* ☐ ☐ ☐

The leader demonstrates a strong understanding of each individual. This is a strong grasp of emotional intelligence.

Comment: _____

Additional Comments & Feedback: _____

_____

_____

_____

_____

_____

_____

As one of Ann's mentors, and being the one who worked with Ann on her original Leadership Traits Evaluation, I drafted an email to the repeat participants defining our request and timeline of completion. Next, Ann and I drafted an email to her additional mentors, peers from outside our organization, and the two individuals whom she was mentoring, explaining the request and process along with the timeline of completion. I drafted schedule reminders, which were easy to have prepared, to send to those whose response was still needed. After two days, and according to the timeline, each person had returned their completed evaluation with comments. Ann and I scheduled the next business morning to review them.

Ann and I met the next morning in one of our conference rooms. I reminded Ann that humility is a strength and that we need solid and honest feedback that will allow her to absorb, understand, and grow from. In all my years of coaching leadership, I have always circled back to this fact. As a review, we determined each trait to be assessed, as we did in the beginning, to ensure a clear understanding of each trait. Ann and I reviewed the categories of scoring, 1. Needs Improvement, 2. Meets Standards, 3. Exceeds, and how it is rare to earn a 3 Exceeds. I reviewed why we score this way, even though Ann was familiar with the reasoning and the process. However, it was important for me to explain that in this review we were rating where Ann was regarding her present position and status, which is different from comparing it to her prior assessment. This can be confusing, but because over a year, the expectations were for Ann to develop in her skills and knowledge which advances each trait. So although she may have been a #2 Meets Standards in her original review, the expectation for maintaining a #2 Meets Standards would be with the expected growth, development, and role changes. Growth does not define that they exceeded in this area. To exceed, they must execute above the means of high expectations that truly advanced this area in unexpected ways. I reminded Ann, as I did with the other participants, that a #2 Meets Standards defines that the individual meets our standards as an organization and as a high performer, as we have high expectations to begin with. In the original assessment, Ann and I would utilize some of her examples in understanding a trait and how she measured it. With a year's performance, Ann certainly had work-related and personal examples to help define each trait more clearly.

Vision: In the original review, Ann and I discussed how she shared the vision with her son which allowed her to understand vision more clearly. As her role had expanded within the last year, with her promotion and running a sales team, vision had become more prevalent within her professional environment. Ann's perspective had grown on how she could affect performance through the sharing of a vision, large and small, that demonstrates progress and focus that drives success. Ann had rated herself a #1 Needs Improvement in her original assessment. With today's assessment, and with her new role, she rated herself a #2 Meets Standards. Ann wrote in her comments that she routinely gives updates on progress, large and small, and looks for new ways to keep her team informed. As we started to review from the Leadership 360, from those that assessed her originally within our organization, they rated her a #2 Meets Standards as well. The comments supported Ann's comments stating that she constantly shared wins, large and small, and pointed to progress. It was also stated she had incorporated rhythms within the business that allowed for updates that others shared as she worked to gain the involvement of her team. This was strong and encouraging feedback. As we reviewed the assessments from outside our organization, each spoke to how much Ann had taught them, and how she drives vision within the organizations they are a part of. The trend spoke of her systematic ways of teaching and executing consistently in driving the vision. As Ann and I reviewed, I mentioned to Ann that it demonstrates how much teaching others, as well as sharing with others, has expanded her skill level. Ann agreed, and spoke to the fact that this had become very rewarding and it increased her drive as well.

The next trait on the assessment was communication, which is an important aspect of leadership. We teach in leadership that great leaders over-communicate, and in fact, great leaders repeat themselves in the areas of importance. In contrast, weak leaders avoid communication concerning difficult topics. In times of crisis, a strong leader ensures their visibility and communication are at the forefront. In her original assessment, Ann rated herself a #2 Meets Standards. As she met high standards for the position she held. With the new position, and her growth and development, Ann rated herself #2 Meet Standards as she believed she still met the high expectations required. She wrote in her comments that as she had developed her Emotional Intelligence that she communicates more effectively by understanding better the makeup of each individual she communicates with. Also, she has read and incorporated some tactics, knowledge, and skills from books like *The Rockefeller Habits*, and others. This was validated by assessments from those within our organization, as well as those outside our organization. In fact, from one outside our organization, Ann and

I laughed when we read the comment that Ann repeats herself, and explains to them why she does. Another individual stated that even through difficult situations, they are never at a loss for the ability to communicate with Ann.

Decisiveness was the next trait on the assessment. Weak leaders lack decisiveness and strong leaders build a decision-making process that enhances their ability to be confident and decisive. Being decisive is not making quick decisions with no guidance. Being decisive is having built a process and habit of problem-solving and decision-making that enables decisiveness as the result. Decision-making becomes natural and the decisions are well-balanced. Ann once again had rated herself a #2 Meets Standards in her original

> *Being decisive is having built a process and habit of problem-solving and decision-making that enables decisiveness as the result.*

assessment, and rated herself the same with the new role with her advanced skills and knowledge. She commented that she had a decision-making roadmap on her office wall and taught her team the same process. The feedback received from those within our organization, especially direct reports, stated that Ann taught her team to be problem-solvers and to bring solutions and ideas when they need assistance. It was stated how much this was appreciated. One commented on how consistent Ann was when problems were brought to her, on what questions she asked or what data she desired, and that their decision-making process had advanced through participation. Assessments from outside our organization spoke about how Ann shared her decision-making process, but was open to learning other resources shared by others. This is encouraging as understanding that there are other methods and learning about them only increases innovation and creativity. I inserted a comment for recommended reading for Ann.

Trust and integrity are important key areas as a leader must demonstrate and earn this daily. Leaders need to understand that they are being watched at all times, and measured by their actions. Trust and integrity are difficult to earn back if lost. Ann rated herself a #2 Meets Standards in her original assessment and rated herself the same with the current assessment. She wrote in her comments that she works on transparency, and demonstrated honesty professionally, even if painful, for the benefit of everyone. In the review received within our organization, several scored Ann a #3 Exceeds Standards with one giving her a #2 Meets Standards. The comments given were admirable as each stated how Ann stood on strong standards of integrity and honesty, and one even gave an example of Ann correcting a contest in which the team had won, but the correction gave the victory to another team. Although no one may have caught the error, the data was incorrect, and Ann had to stand on this principle, as well as expect the same from her team. Although this may have disgruntled some, they too understood and developed higher standards from the experience. The assessments from outside our organization stated the same beliefs, as she received #2 Meets Standards and #3 Exceeds Standards from them.

Inspiration was the next trait of the assessment. Much like the others, Ann rated herself a #2 Meets Standards in her original assessment, and a #2 Meets Standards with the current assessment. What Ann believed improved was her understanding of ways she can be proactive in regards to inspiring others. She wrote in her comments that she had read *The One Minute Manager* which was recommended, expanded to other books, and even attended a workshop. Ann was rated the same by both inside and outside our organization as a #2 Meets Standards on the assessment. However, both spoke and commented that they followed Ann, and utilized this terminology because she inspired them to succeed, develop, and reach for higher levels of success. One individual she was mentoring commented that they witnessed Ann with others and wanted to learn from her due to her inspiration. They mentioned that Ann had a waiting list of those that desired her mentorship. Ann was defining ways on how she could assist others without spreading herself too thin. She and I had planned to discuss this separately.

Optimism is a trait where others have stated that Ann is the biggest cheerleader. This is a portion of the trait, but optimism runs a little deeper. It is strategic in how one develops plans and initiatives that allow for transparency, so that all can see tangible progress easily. This is how leaders demonstrate that their optimism is realistic. A leader who always states things can be accomplished and then consistently fails, will soon have others that don't believe in their optimism. Great leaders whose optimism is supported by a track record of success gain followers, even if a failure or two occurs. This is because an optimistic leader is not afraid of failure, but demonstrates what failure teaches. Ann rate herself a #2 Meets Standards originally and rated herself the same with the current assessment. She commented once again of learning from *The One Minute Manager,* but spoke to some additional books as well. The assessments from our organization spoke well and measured her a #2 Meets Standards. The comments about her optimism were rewarding as one noted an example of when the team missed a goal and how Ann quickly gathered the team, broke down the failure, and re-established a new goal in which they exceeded. So, through failure, her optimism kept her active where others may have accepted the failure. Much the same feedback came from the assessments from outside our organization as those from her support network commented that Ann's optimism is proactive, as she demonstrates that she goes out of her way to seek how she can assist them.

Facilitation was a trait Ann believed she needed improvement on from the past, so in her original assessment, she scored herself a #1 Needs Improvement. Remember, facilitation is not just about running and conducting meetings. Facilitation is that the leader has a strong ability to lead and facilitate their team and others to focus on goal achievement. Facilitation skills are something used by someone who can guide and direct others with the skill of allowing them to come to a proper conclusion while taking them through the process. The skill allows the individuals to be taught to learn while executing and to draw their own conclusion. However, the facilitator has the skill to help direct them to what is determined as being the proper conclusion. This is how a leader coaches and educates. Ann then rated herself a #2 Meets Standards and wrote in her comments that she had developed this through a few courses and within action steps. The first step she listed is how she was teaching her team problem-solving skills, as she facilitated them through the process to find the proper conclusions. Ann could easily decide for them, but through facilitation she educated them. In the process, problem-solving becomes natural to them and enhances the team's strengths. She had expanded this to how she coached sales personnel through the sales process with a client, so through facilitation, their thought process developed and skills improved. The feedback from direct reports from our organization agreed, as everyone rated her a #2 Meets Standards, and made reference to the same comments that Ann listed. However, the outside assessments also rated her a #2 Meets Standards, and the comments stated she was gifted at working them through systems and processes to define a proper conclusion. This was powerful feedback and even surprised Ann.

Commitment and passion were the next two traits that were listed together. In Ann's original assessment, she spoke of her immediate supervisor's commitment and passion, and how his commitment allowed him to expect more from his team, which he drove through his passion. Ann also demonstrated passion for her role at the time, which was recognized by those she served. She scored herself a #2 Meets Standards on both assessments. In our discussion, Ann stated that she realized that with her promotion and leadership of a team, that leadership and passion are a higher level of responsibility. With that new responsibility she had worked hard to maintain a #2 Meets Standards in her current role. She worked with her team members to define a career path for each and showed a passion by her commitments to each individual having access to the tools for advancing. She further demonstrated a commitment to passion by demonstrating self-accountability and pushing the accountability of her team. The responses and feedback from her assessments, both from our organization and from her support network, rated Ann a #2 Meets Standards. However, both spoke to how Ann's commitment and passion created a higher level of self-accountability within them that drove their commitment and passion individually.

Accountability follows as the next trait in the assessment for a reason. In her original assessment, Ann spoke of how her immediate supervisor would teach on self-accountability and its importance. From the comments on the traits of commitment and passion, we can see how this drives all-around accountability. However, strong leaders speak to accountability proactively, consistently, and openly. Ann had a goal of reading *The Rockefeller Habits,* which teaches tools to manage accountability with measures. She read this book with me as her mentor and in the discussion, she had mentioned that she learned from the book each time she used it in mentoring others. Her score on the original assessment was a #2 Meets Standards and with her higher level of responsibility with her leadership promotion, Ann rated herself a #2 Meets Standards at this time too. Ann's direct reports from our organization rated Ann a #2 Meets Standards, with a couple rating her a #3 Exceeds. They spoke on how Ann had created new methods and reports that proactively raise the level of accountability through her systems and processes. Her assessments from her outside contacts, her support network, rated her a #2 Meets Standards and had shared comments on how she taught and demonstrated systems and processes and how they aided in accountability.

Empowerment was a trait that when we arrived on it to discuss, Ann mentioned how managing a team had allowed her to comprehend the power behind empowerment, and how this had assisted in her coaching her team members to be problem-solvers. We discussed how she had learned to define parameters in each of their roles of decision-making and expected tasks and accountability. Ann stated, that at times that she had been empowered, she had embraced it as it catapulted her growth. In her original assessment, she rated herself a #2 Meets Standards as at that time she sought empowerment and the accountability that came with it. With her promotion, she had realized that empowerment is a great leadership tool in developing others, as well as in gaining and earning trust. We discussed what she learned in our reading of the book, *The Speed of Trust*, and the values that it teaches. Her team assessed her a #3 Exceeds, with each one listing examples on how Ann utilized empowerment with each of them individually. She had utilized Emotional Intelligence in understanding how each one would respond with different techniques of empowerment. Her support network assessment rated her a #2 Meets Standards with high praises. However, the rating of a #3 Exceeds from her internal team demonstrated this is a key area of strength for Ann from those that report directly to her. This was a strong compliment.

Creativity and innovation are strong traits for Ann as well as the next to be assessed. In her original role and assessment, Ann rated herself a #2 Meets Standards. However, within that role is where her skills for leadership were discovered and creativity and innovation played a big role. She created new reports that helped manage progress and measure success. She also grasped innovative ways our systems could improve the effectiveness of our workforce. I had recommended to Ann the book *Blue Ocean Strategy* to learn more about innovation and thinking outside the box. It is one that she had not read as of yet, as others were listed to read first. In the current assessment, Ann rated herself a #2 Meets Standards. She stated that with the promotion she recognized growth was needed to be able to coach and develop a team to strive on creativity and innovation by sharing their ideas, but also by embracing change. She additionally wrote in her comments that she would not only read *Blue Ocean Strategy*, but add other materials that taught about not taking shortcuts, which is a balance when incorporating creativity and innovation. Assessments from our organization, as well as from Ann's support network, both rated Ann a #2 Meets Standards. The comments from our organization mentioned how Ann had built an environment to express new ideas and that it was okay to challenge the status quo. From her support network, the feedback was that Ann would encourage thinking of solutions in a Plan A and Plan B methodology.

Empathy is an area that Ann rated herself a #2 Meet Standards in her original assessment. She comprehended the concept of Emotional Intelligence and its relationship in understanding empathy and how each individual reacts differently. On the current assessment, she rated herself a #2 Meets Standards. She listed in her comments the course she took on Emotional Intelligence, as well as how she comprehends the 5-components that make up the EQ measurement of Emotional Intelligence. Ann learned that Emotional Intelligence can be improved, as well as the techniques for improving them. Also, Ann had training delivered on Emotional Intelligence for her team, with a one-day workshop. This paid dividends with their understanding, but also her team learning how they can improve their Emotional Intelligence. As with any training, it also allowed Ann to measure which individual members grow and develop further, and which ones take an interest in improving. Ann's assessments from her team within our organization rated her a #2 Meets Standards, and many comments stated they appreciated how she related to them, as well as their appreciation of the training. Ann's outside group, her support network, rated her a #2 Meets Standards as well. It is mentioned by those she mentored how Ann had introduced them to Emotional Intelligence and an assessment that measures their EQ. Her mentors and peers in the groups spoke to how they provided feedback and accountability to each other and were honest about their individual growth and challenges. This is a testament to working with a solid peer group.

Ann and I completed assessing the reviews and noted the comments. We discussed any items that either of us needed clarity on. I asked Ann to gather her thoughts together in regards to this evaluation, define what she learned, what surprised her, and what changes that would drive. This is an important aspect as sometimes the evaluations may show you are progressing well and on the right track. Other times the evaluation may show a lack of progress or a discrepancy in a key area. If there are differences of opinion on any area, it is important to understand what drove the other perception and if it has validity. It is with these answers that one can then determine what changes and adjustments can be made, or should be made. If one believes or defines wholesale changes that need to be made, that would be a concern. Hopefully, it is a guide to small adjustments that help make an impact. I provided Ann a worksheet to assist her in determining her thoughts. The sheet asks simple questions, that when answering can spark the thought process, especially in defining how to advance certain traits. We agreed on a time to meet the next day.

• • • • • • • • • • •

If there are differences of opinion on any area, it is important to understand what drove the other perception and if it has validity.

• • • • • • • • • • •

Mark Villareal
People, Strategy, Execution

Leadership Traits Evaluation Questionnaire

1. When evaluating your assessments, what trait did you make the most growth in from your last Leadership Traits Evaluation? Define the growth.

   _____

   _____

   _____

   _____

   _____

2. What trait, if any, did you score #1 Needs Improvement from your last Leadership Traits Evaluation and what growth did you show based on the recent assessments?

   _____

   _____

   _____

   _____

3. Define the changes, if any, in your role, growth, responsibilities, and accountability from your last Leadership Traits Evaluation as compared to your recent one?

   _____

   _____

   _____

   _____

   _____

4. How does your answer in Question #3 affect your outlook for your most recent Leadership Traits Evaluation?

_____

_____

_____

_____

_____

_____

_____

5. What trait, if any, was there any discrepancy from peers or others from your own assessment on your current Leadership Traits Evaluation? Define if they matched, or any discrepancies and your thought process on why the discrepancy?

_____

_____

_____

_____

_____

_____

6. Which trait development offers you the most rewards? Define:

_____

_____

_____

_____

_____

_____

7. What trait development causes you any concern or roadblock? Define:

_____

_____

_____

_____

_____

8. Which trait from your Leadership Traits Evaluation assessment and mindset are you most critical about yourself? Define:

_____

_____

_____

_____

_____

9. Which trait, do you define, as one that can make a significant impact? Why?

_____

_____

_____

_____

10. What recommendations and feedback from your Leadership Traits Evaluation 360 add value and insight? Define:

_____

_____

_____

_____

11. If you could have accomplished more in any one trait between evaluations, which trait is it and what hindered progress, or could have accelerated progress?

_____

_____

_____

_____

_____

12. What accomplishment are you most pleased with? Define:

_____

_____

_____

_____

_____

13. What area or trait, are you discouraged with, if at all? Define:

_____

_____

_____

_____

_____

14. What surprised you about the Leadership Traits Evaluation 360 process and how would you improve it?

_____

_____

_____

_____

15. Describe your experience through the process and what additional information you learned.

_____

_____

_____

_____

_____

_____

Ann and I met the next day in the same conference room. Ann had completed the questionnaire I gave her as I could see her handwriting on the document. This would allow us to discuss the Leadership Traits Evaluation 360, from her perspective, having reviewed the feedback of others. What helps a person gain a more complete perspective is the review itself and then a little reflection of the process. I find this valuable even if everyone is on the same page. Gaining and resetting a foundational mindset allows a person to move forward with confidence and with a solid focus on their objectives. Ann was already in the conference room when I arrived.

"Hello, Ann," I greeted, as I entered the room.

"Good morning," she replied. Ann handed me a copy of the questionnaire as I sat down.

"How did you find the questionnaire?" I asked.

"I found it thought-provoking," she replied. "I did not find it challenging, but I did like that it made me think with each question on my perspective and the feedback from the 360. I could understand that the intent is to help one gain a clear understanding of where they stand, how they are doing, and allow insight into the next steps."

"Yes," I responded. "With this evaluation being a one-year evaluation, we are still in the middle of many of the goals and objectives. So this allows for a reflection to measure if you are still on the execution path of those goals and objectives, and what, if anything, needs adjustment. One may find they need to push harder in one area and I have seen a few times where one might adjust a goal or objective or add a new one altogether."

"It does bring a lot of reflection into what you have committed to, and the actual execution," Ann mused. "It caused some soul-searching in an area or two and I questioned my inner-hunger of what I want to achieve. It is important that I still believe and have the desire."

"Exactly," I replied. "It sounds like it allowed you to test your foundation and your outlook on your objectives and goals?"

"Yes, it did," she replied. "This is where the value of the exercise is. It brought me back to ensure my foundation is firm."

"Great," I continued. "Then let's review the questionnaire."

I pulled the copy that Ann supplied, and although it had her written answers, I wanted to review each question and then ask her to read her answer. From there, we could expand on her answers and her thoughts that arose.

"Number one," I started. "When evaluating your assessments, what trait did you make the most growth in from your last Leadership Traits Evaluation? Define the growth."

Ann lifted her copy and was about to start reading, but then lowered her arm to make a statement. "Here is what I found interesting. At first, my automatic answer may have been vision, as that is where in my original assessment I rated myself a #1 Needs Improvement. And with this evaluation, I have rated myself a #2 Meets Standards, which demonstrates growth. However, with my growth and development, as well as changes to my role, expectations have risen. So as I gave it additional thought, communication is the trait that I believe I have grown most and expanded most. I have discovered the importance of communication, and how it is tied to other traits. When developed, effectively good communication is important. Strong communication makes an impact, especially with emotional intelligence, accountability, decisiveness, and empowerment. Had I not developed stronger communication skills and tactics, I would not have developed better empowerment."

"That is great insight," I commented. "Although you were a #2 Meets Standards both times in your assessments, it is expectations of growth within your existing role, and with the role change, that further development is needed. Because of high expectations and with growth, development, and role changes, a person could slide if their development in the trait does not grow equally with everything else. This is a key point in understanding and explaining to those you will mentor. It is important for the person who is being assessed to realize how the dynamics and expectations become higher and harder, and a #2 Meet Standards rise with it."

"That is so true!" she exclaimed.

This allowed me to see where having mentors is important. Good mentors speak the truth and bring an understanding of higher expectations.

"Okay," I said, as I lifted the questionnaire to read, "Number two, what trait, if any, did you score #1 Needs Improvement from your last Leadership Traits Evaluation and what growth did you show based on the recent assessments?"

Ann laughed a little as she spoke. "This is what we just mentioned. Vision, last time I scored myself a #1 Needs Improvement. Others as well scored me the same although the feedback was positive and encouraging. But executing the original assessment alone, I received an education and insight to comprehend more on vision and how in many ways I was demonstrating vision already. But now with my studies, like reading the *Rockefeller Habits* and with working in my support network, I have learned not only how to be proactive in sharing vision, but also pointing to the milestones that build-up to the small victories leading to achievements that drive a team in believing they will obtain the vision. I look forward to developing further, as with any trait you can grow and develop more."

"Yes, that is a great insight," I replied. "Great leaders share the vision constantly. They point to those small wins and lead everyone forward. You also mention facilitation in your notes. What is your feedback on facilitation?"

"Facilitation, I rated myself a #1 Needs Improvement in my original assessment. I needed more exposure to ways to facilitate proactively and consistently. Also, as I embrace systems and processes this opens the door for me to facilitate the learning of others. I believe that having been proactive this has worked strongly in my favor." Ann sighed, as she was excited about her progress.

"I could not agree more," I state with encouragement. "Now, number three, define the changes, if any, in your role, growth, responsibilities, and accountability from your last Leadership Traits Evaluation as compared to your recent one?"

Ann answered, "I wrote, I have assumed additional responsibilities and a higher level of accountability. I now lead a small sales team that with success and development will grow in its size and expectations. I have revenue expectations, profitability account-ability, as well as personnel development requirements."

"Number four is a follow up to number three," I spoke. "How does your answer in Question #3 affect your outlook for your most recent Leadership Traits Evaluation?"

Ann paused before she spoke. "I like how this makes you think about your growth along with the increased expectations that come with the additional responsibilities."

"That is the value of evaluating, to reflect, and to understand that as you grow you have a greater responsibility," I defined.

Ann nodded her head in agreement. "Here is what I wrote. My outlook is a realization that I must look for opportunities to increase my accountability and responsibilities. As my role grows, I must be proactive in the development of others, and raise the expectations of those I lead. I understand the importance of lead, follow, or get out of the way."

"Very good," I said complimentary. "You can see that as you grow, those around you must grow. Those that relax will be passed by. Let's move on to number five. What trait, if any, was there any discrepancy from peers or others from your own assessment on your current Leadership Traits Evaluation? Define if they matched, or any discrepancies and your thought process on why the discrepancy?"

"Here I reviewed a couple," Ann began. "Empowerment was the one that although I rated myself a #2 Meets Standards, many of my direct reports rated me a #3 Exceeds. I guess this is a positive as we could be discussing an example of them rating me lower than myself." Ann paused and laughed. "However, their comments demonstrate the discrepancy arose from the tools and skills I utilized like earning trust and my development of emotional intelligence. I was unaware of how they viewed or recognized these areas, and more importantly, placed value on them."

"You will learn in leadership that those you lead will surprise you on how they understand your strengths and tactics and appreciate the leader for using them," I explained.

"That is so true," Ann responded.

"Number six, which trait development offers you the most rewards?" I asked.

Ann spoke, quickly. "Empowerment!" She laughed. "Funny, but at different moments the answer could be different traits. But I witnessed how empowerment has grown our team and developed individuals in their skills and knowledge."

"I believe helping individuals grow and develop is very rewarding," I commented. "Let's go to number seven, what trait development causes you any concern or roadblock?"

"Here is where I separated innovation," Ann answered. "This was part of creativity and my assessment demonstrates I do well in work tasks and improvements, but innovation outside the box is where I need growth and a better understanding. I can take items already within my purview and be more creative with them. But to have the advanced skill to grasp things outside my purview and be innovative in building new revenue streams is my next challenge. At some point, great companies reinvent themselves and I want to be part of that."

I was impressed with Ann's answer. "Ann, I believe you have given this solid insight and to be innovative is important. There is always a balance between what is outside the box and what is already in the box when defining new ideas. But for organizations to grow, they need innovation that creates new revenue streams and new ways of providing their services and product. I know we have *Blue Ocean Strategy* on your reading list, so let's make sure we read through the book in the next quarter. However, it is important to note and to realize that for innovation to be strong, the individual must be strong in the other traits first. This is why we worked on those in our mentoring sessions as these traits support innovation. They are the foundation for the execution and success of innovative ideas."

* * * * * * * * * * * *

For innovation to be strong, the individual must be strong in the other traits first.

* * * * * * * * * * * *

"I can understand that perspective," Ann replied. "Accountability has to be solid, as well as decisiveness with a solid decision-making process. I see where empowerment plays a big role, as innovation must have others involved. We certainly could name each trait and its significance."

"We certainly can," I responded. "This is why we do these sessions and evaluations, as these discussions add to the learning. We are on number eight, which trait from your Leadership Traits Evaluation assessment and mindset are you most critical about yourself?"

"Decisiveness," Ann answered, quickly. We laughed because she said it so decisively. "This is a trait that I have learned a leader always needs to work on, learn more knowledge, and increase their skills in. It is almost like decisiveness is a muscle, and we must keep it in shape and exercise it regularly. By learning other methods of decision-making, has helped me to learn that problems can be addressed from different viewpoints. I have worked on pausing when others have a different point of view, so that I can hear them. It is important to grow others along the way. But it should never stop."

"Ann, decisiveness is a good trait to be critical on," I commented. "I agree that you must exercise your decisiveness muscle to stay in shape. Good insight. Now let's go to number nine, which trait do you define as one that can make a significant impact?"

"This question I could answer differently based upon different days and circumstances," Ann answered. "However, accountability is my answer. This is because I see my team is at the tipping point of development with the ability to rise to the next level. So accountability to our results, development, and organization is imperative for their benefit and growth."

"Yes, I agree, that based upon circumstance and timing the answer could be different. But your team is on the cusp of greater things, and accountability is key. We are on number ten, what recommendations and feedback from your Leadership Traits Evaluation 360 add value and insight?"

"I value all the insight," she replied. "I take each comment to heart to see how it can improve me. I did find value and validation on the feedback on optimism, where I confronted our team missing a goal immediately, and with optimism, set correction and actions for us to execute and rise above the challenge. Hearing the feedback allowed me to understand that the actions had an impact."

"That is true, that sometimes the validation through comments means everything," I commented. "We are now on number eleven, if you could have accomplished more in any one trait between evaluations, which trait is it and what hindered progress, or could have accelerated progress?"

"Here is where I mentioned innovation before," Ann answered. "Certainly, I know I could have grown more, but I also understand that I was not hindered. It is that other traits development took priority and had a greater impact on the stage that I was at. I comprehend the process more clearly now and appreciate it."

"Very true in your comprehension. If there was a good design for your growth and development that allows you to learn best, it is what we designed. Certainly, we had an adjustment or two, that is why we evaluate. But developing leaders must have a pecking order of development," I stated.

"Yes, I see that now," Ann acknowledged. "Of course, at different times we believe we can learn and do all things at once. But that would stunt our development."

I nodded my head in agreement. "You are correct. Let's move on to question number twelve. What accomplishment are you most pleased with?"

"Commitment and passion are what I answered," she stated. "I answered this way because I kept high standards in this area in a trying environment where this can easily slip, even for a moment. I am pleased that peers and direct reports had similar views and recognized my passion for their development. So my biggest worry is to be viewed as it is all about me, which it is not. I make an effort to show it is all about others, as well as their growth and development. I believe in the philosophy that you have taught your leaders, that the more you focus on others' success yours will come naturally. I am pleased that I can demonstrate that too."

"Awesome," I blurted. "You certainly know and understand servant leadership. This will serve you well. Question number thirteen, what area or trait, are you discouraged with, if at all?"

Ann hesitated and grimaced. "Do I have to have an answer? You can see I left this one blank. I am not discouraged on any of them, at this moment. I certainly know and understand that I always need to learn and develop, but none of them discourage me."

I laughed for a moment. "No, you do not have to have an answer. Actually what you answered is an answer and a valid one at that. Question fourteen, what surprised you about the Leadership Traits Evaluation 360 process and how would you improve it?"

"This I gave some thought to," Ann answered. "I was surprised by everyone's willingness to participate and in their candor. Now I believe this is due to the environment that is created at our organization, but I also saw this from my support network. The only thoughts of adding or improving would be a scenario where those that participate all come together in the same room and we would walk through each evaluation. That would be powerful."

"That would be powerful and I have participated in such a scenario. We have utilized it with higher-level leaders where the coordination was easier and the participants had the relationship and comfort level of being present to express their feedback with candor. There is a lot of trust and vulnerability in such a session," I explained.

"I would imagine so," Ann stated.

"Okay," I said. "We are on number fifteen. Describe your experience through the process and what additional information you learned."

Ann lifted her copy to read and then set her arm down to speak. "Mark, I have learned that I belong, that I too am a leader. The process teaches and builds self-confidence, and also builds a desire for growth and development. To allow yourself to be vulnerable, at first, is difficult. But then you want others' feedback and candor as you realize that it is important for your growth."

"Ann, I appreciate your feedback and I appreciate you," I responded. "You certainly have grown and developed and I see by your results that you are paying it forward, which is a true measure of a leader. Now that we have completed this, we will next review your personal and professional goals you have listed and see how you are doing. Then, finally, we will review your Development Plan to ensure you are on plan, or to add and make any adjustments."

"Okay, thanks," Ann replied.

Evaluating Ann's Personal and Professional Goals:

As a mentor, and as a leader, I find power in helping others define their personal and professional goals, as both are key to growth as they intertwine with each other. I remember that in the past it may have been taboo to ask a person about their personal goals in a work environment. However, my firm belief is understanding an individual's personal goals assists in defining their professional goals, as both sets of goals are catalysts on driving results and achievement. As a leader, I have always enjoyed celebrating an employee's accomplishment, whether personal or professional. Celebrating both sides accelerates the achievement. Mentoring aspiring women in leadership, it is important to understand each and to demonstrate how they tie together. How certain goals are reliant on the achievement of others and understanding how planning can play a role in their success.

When originally defining Ann's Vision Statement, I had Ann define six foundational core goals that helped lay the groundwork. It is from this process we fleshed out additional goals that we then mapped out what skills and knowledge would be needed to help develop Ann for their achievement. Ann and I had scheduled time at her one-year evaluation process that followed our reviews of her Leadership Traits 360. We scheduled on a separate day and met in one of our organization's conference rooms.

Ann walked into the conference room, as I had arrived first. "Good morning, I hope you have not been waiting long."

"No," I replied. "We are on time to start. I like doing this process early in the day, so our mind is clear and fresh."

Ann laughed. "Oh yes, plus I need my coffee!"

"Ann, I would like to start with the six core foundational goals you created when we were defining your Vision Statement."

"Okay," Ann stated.

I pulled out the worksheet she had completed from her file for us to read and discuss, so we could then evaluate progress.

Mark Villareal

People, Strategy, Execution

Foundational Core Goals

Define goals and objectives for each category with a 3 to 5 year outlook. Be specific with each goal. Think of how the goal(s) will be measured and described. Describe if they are a challenge, yet attainable. Give thought if the goal is relevant to your life and your outlook on achievements. Ensure that all goals are time-bound. If you need to list notes to flesh out with a mentor, please list.

1. Family: When I asked Ann for her 3 to 5 year goal for her family, she quickly went to her son. Being a parent helps define your focus. Ann relayed that her goal for her son was to have grades good enough for college and a passion he has defined for a direction for his life. This is a good goal, but I pushed her for more definitions. What type of grades? She replied 3.2 or higher. Then I asked what type of passion. She stated that her desire, and his at the present, was for a degree in chemical engineering, to work in this field or to teach, as he likes helping others. But he would also consider a business degree. So we listed that out as a family goal.

2. Financial: Ann responded that she would like to be financially independent and to own a home. At present, she and her husband had always rented. I pushed deeper on the financial independence and she stated that they had always lived paycheck to paycheck. So I suggested we write a goal with specifics and timelines using the SMART Goal method. We

defined the goal specifics as To own a home in 3-years with the ability to save 15% of income for savings.

3. Physical: Here Ann described that she would like both her and her husband to become active together, as well as to get into shape. I asked what would be the goal of any weight loss? What would be the goal regarding activity? She defined the goal as each losing about 20-pounds and maintaining it, she would like to see that obtained within six months. On activity, she stated her goal would be for each of them to commit to visiting a local gym three times a week, morning or evenings. She would like to see that started and executed consistently within two months, so they can arrange schedules.

4. Mental: Everyone needs to understand that mental fitness is important. Exercising your mental muscle and challenging it will help one with stress and patience. Ann thought about this one a while. She believed that if she could read one book a month, whether for work or enjoyment, but just read and enjoy, that it would help her mentally. She stated that reading relaxed her and allowed her to meditate. This goal was pretty precise, although one can define what types of books to read if they feel the need.

5. Spiritual: On this topic, I always coach that I will not judge, as many have different interpretations of spirituality. But with Ann, hers were more grounded in the Christian faith in which she was raised. She spoke about believing in the faith, but perhaps straying or not being consistent. Her goal was to become part of a bible study that met at least twice a month. She knew her church had those available and wanted to become active within one.

6. Career: Number six is career. She and I would expand on this more within additional exercises. But here is a good opportunity to define an early goal that would help us with her vision. She stated that within three years she would like to be a group manager, which in our business is just above a team lead. So this means she would have to be promoted twice within two years. While achievable, it is a little aggressive.

"What I would like to do, Ann, is for us to read them, and since most have a 3 to 5 year outlook I want us to identify if you are still on track. Also, is there anything of concern, or roadblocks that we can address? And finally, anything to add?" I explained.

Ann started reading them to herself, as I reviewed the copy I had. "I believe the first one on family, which speaks about my son, is still on track. Thankfully, his grades are still on track. However, I would add for us to have a set time for a vacation, or parameters for a time that the family will always take a yearly vacation to spend time together. Also, my husband and I have created a date night for us once per week. These are important because with the extra effort and goals it takes time away, so a commitment on when we spend time together demonstrates its importance."

"Ann, those are excellent additions. I am glad that you and your family have seen how to work around the extra commitments to drive the importance of family," I praised.

Ann read number two to herself. "The financial personal goal will remain the same. We are making more and saving some, but not consistently, so that needs to get better. Although I have taken a course on personal finance, my husband and I are now taking one with our church. This one is to teach us better habits, which should help."

"The fact that you are taking this together adds tremendous value. In a marriage, good habits are best when both are aware and understand the why behind the habit. You are working together instead of against each other," I commented.

Ann nodded her head in agreement. "I am surprised by how much we look forward to it. Learning together will help us remind each other. The next goal, being physical, is one we are doing better at. However, we discussed how to make it more fun, like when on vacation to go hiking. We also added bike riding in the park. That is what I would add."

"Very good," I replied "Yes, some may see physical as demanding, and resent it. To add fun to it is smart. What about the goal in the mental category?"

Ann responded, "On mental, I would keep the same. Although I would expand with watching documentaries with my husband. It is something we do about two times per month and we enjoy it. We started with history, but have expanded it to National Parks which has driven our desire to vacations."

"Okay, we can add that," I agreed. "What about spiritual?"

Ann answered, quickly. "Here we just need to stay consistent. I would keep the goal the same, but add the word consistently."

"Okay," I replied. "Now, the last one is career. This one you are doing well and on pace for. Are there any concerns or anything else you would like to add?"

"I do appear on plan," Ann agreed. "However, I would like to add to have developed two new leaders within the two years. So this makes the goal more than just about me."

"Great, yes, adding that will also make you realize that as you develop others, you create your own promotion. You get recognized quickly," I commented.

After this, we went into reviewing and evaluating Ann's long-term goals, to ensure she was still on plan. Her long-term goals were created for a 5 to 10 year outlook, so at a one-year evaluation we can test that they are still on plan and not off track. We can ask if they are even started. Ann appeared on plan as her long-term goals were owning a home, two rental properties, and a 401K investment of 200k after 20-years. She joined the 401k program that year and had a standard 10% withdrawal that was teaching her the habit of living off the rest. It is from her long-term goals that we defined 10 short-term goals for personal development that map to her achieving her long-term success and coincide with professional success. Also, we mapped out 4 professional development goals that the personal goals benefit from the growth of each one. This helps create success for personal and professional environments.

I handed Ann the list we created on her short-term goals so we could walk through each, and then evaluate.

Mark Villareal
People, Strategy, Execution

Personal Development Goals

Break down your long-term goals, both personal and professional, to determine what short-term development goals in skills and knowledge are needed for their achievement. Keep a mindset that these goals are a 1 to 2-year outlook for completion. It is highly recommended to work with a mentor who has achieved success personally as well as professionally.

List Personal Short-Term Development Goals (up to 10):

1. Financial Management – Understanding personal finance and investment.
2. Empathy (Emotional Intelligence) – developing and managing the understanding of an individual's different make-ups.
3. Communication – Developing the skills of effective communication, tied with the knowledge of Emotional Intelligence.
4. Persuasion / Influence – To learn the skills and knowledge to persuade and influence others as a leader that gains commitment and followers.
5. Assertiveness – To learn that confrontation is a benefit and how to be assertive effectively so that others maintain mutual respect.
6. Habits – To define, learn, and consistently put forth good habits that drive good results and accountability.

7. Overcoming Adversity / Resilience – To gain the ability to face, overcome, and flourish through adversity. To demonstrate resilience when working through obstacles and setbacks.

9. Decision-Making – To define a proper method of decision-making that brings the right solutions. To be consistent and decisive with confidence.

10. Listening Skills – To be an effective listener, showing proper focus and attention that earns respect and demonstrates the importance of gaining understanding.

List Professional Short-Term Development Goals (Approximately 4)

1. Change Management – To develop the leadership skills that demonstrate effective change management that leads a team through proper change achieving the objective and outcome.

2. Conflict Resolution – To understand and comprehend proper conflict resolution, and develop the skills to implement with teams and individuals.

3. Trust – To learn the importance and different aspects of trust that earns trust daily, and teaches others to do the same.

4. Humility – To always lead with humility, to be a servant leader and while learning from others and understanding different viewpoints.

I coached Ann that we would read each one to determine if she is still on pace within her development plan with each one. If any area is off-plan or needs additional focus, then the plan should be adjusted. Finally, and after the review of each existing one, Ann and I needed to then define if any additional items of development needed to be added. She understood the process.

"Okay, let's start," I began. "Financial Management is the first one. On your development plan, we listed a course for you to understand business financial management. This is to understand profit and loss statements, balance sheets, along with all things that drive and help manage a business. Of course on the personal side, your needs were the understanding of personal financial management. This includes managing personal finances, but also investment, savings, and tax implications. So with this we mapped out several items on your development plan. You attended an online course I recommended on understanding financial management, and you also took a course at the North Chamber on business financial management. You have done well on those. I also know you took a course on personal financial management with Our Empowering Women, and now you and your husband are taking a course at your church on financial management. With all this, what is your perception, and what else do you believe you need in this area?"

Ann thought for a moment and then responded. "On each side, I would state that I have accomplished staying on plan. Both personal and professional finance I have learned, but the biggest thing that is helping me now on the professional side is the monthly reviews we do with our current financials from our organization. Learning in courses was important, but then seeing them in an actual business drives it home. I will ask that we continue these and at some point be asked to present on a certain section when we do the review. This would test me to show understanding and gain experience by preparing."

"I love the idea!" I exclaimed. "Let's add that to the plan. I also have some more eLearning on building budgets, which I will assign to you. Now, the next one is Empathy, which expands into Emotional Intelligence. Tell me your perspective on this one?"

Ann acknowledged the eLearning course with a nod of her head as she listened to my question. "On Emotional Intelligence I completed the course assigned. I passed the one at the night college course at 90%. I have the 8 Exercises to Increase EQ scheduled to take. I believe I am doing well with my team too, but will always look to improve."

I agreed. "I will look for more in the reading aspect, but for now will comment that you are on plan. Let's move on to Communication Development."

"Okay," Ann stated. "Here, I completed the Dale Carnegie Course above the required percentage. I am near completion of the negotiation course and enjoying the material. The feedback has been positive and constructive. So I am on plan, but believe we will need to add some additional soon."

"Okay, I agree you have done well," I continued. "But when you complete the negotiation course let's look at some reading material and have it defined by Q1 of next year. I will write this in the notes."

Ann acknowledged with a head nod. "Next is Persuasion / Influence. These two courses are the same ones listed for Communication. So I am on plan."

"I will note you are on plan, but with the same notation on Communication. We will look for additional reading materials," I responded.

Ann spoke, "The next one is assertiveness. Here we are doing the coaching one on one. But I have also worked on this with an Our Empowering Women work group, which we need to list here."

I wrote this down for Ann to add to her Development Plan. "Make sure you list the completion date. I also want to add a book to read on professional assertiveness." I briefly went to Amazon on my cell phone and showed Ann the book. We noted this for the plan.

"I like how we are adding additional items," Ann commented. "It demonstrates that development is continuous."

• • • • • • • • • • •

A Development Plan is a living and breathing document when executed properly.

• • • • • • • • • • •

"Exactly," I replied. "A Development Plan is a living and breathing document when executed properly. The next item is Habits."

Ann spoke, quickly, "There are two items on the list and each has been accomplished. I have advanced this by breaking down the *7-Habits of Highly Effective People* for my sales team to demonstrate how they work. This is still developing."

"Great," I exclaimed. "Let's add that to the plan and for us to assess progress in 90-days. Teaching others will demonstrate good progress."

Ann took note to add on to the plan. Ann and I worked down the list, addressing each item, making comments, adjustments if needed, and more importantly adding additional training items so each skill could continue to develop further. When it came to Change Management and Conflict Resolution, Ann and I agreed she was on plan. However, the concern I expressed was that Ann had not encountered or been exposed to enough Change Management or Conflict Resolution, and this is an area where we can work on expanded development. I asked a mentor of mine and he made some strong recommendations which I took back and communicated with Ann. We then included them on the plan.

Values & Principles: (The 3 to 5 Year Mark)

I explained to Ann, that values and principles should be defined as a foundation, and when the individual approves of their values and principles, the review process is usually 3 to 5 years from the creation. Ann remembered the conversation.

"Values and principles can last for a long time for an individual," I explained to Ann. "Usually because values and principles are foundational. However, sometimes because of developmental, personal and professional changes, business associations, as well as mentors and social associations, an individual may determine that it is desirable to evaluate and assess their current values and principles."

"How often should one evaluate?" Ann asked.

"Once you have defined the foundational values and principles, I recommend a re-evaluation and assessment process every 3 to 5 years," I answered. "This I recommend for businesses too. As you grow and execute your plans, and new ones are developed, you may discover that with your growth new values present themselves, or current ones need to adjust or be expanded."

"How does the evaluation process work?" Ann further inquired.

I responded, "The evaluation process allows the assessment of each value, as many may still support and define the individual, but one or two may be determined to need changing for new ones. An assessment is a simple survey with questions that you, as the individual, answer. Also, since you have developed strong relationships with mentors and peers you may ask them to do the same."

"Okay," Ann answered. "Similar to the assessment process on leadership, and others like that?"

"Yes," I stated, matter-of-factly. "I suggest you as the individual execute the assessment first. Then determine what your perception is. From that point, you can define if you would like to involve a mentor or several mentors."

"Do you have an assessment you can share?" Ann asked.

"Yes, I do," I replied. "I have an outline that I can share, and we can discuss what each question means, and what you need to define. Remember, you may find you need to change nothing. But you need to assess if your values and principles are stale, or truly active."

"Thanks," Ann said, cheerfully.

I pulled out the document for Ann and me to review.

Mark Villareal
People. Strategy. Execution

Survey / Assessment—Values & Principles

Please answer the questions on this survey. Use all the space necessary as your feedback is greatly appreciated. Please be professional, yet forthright. Your comments and answers will be confidential.

1. What are your current listed values?

   _____

   _____

   _____

   _____

2. Through example, what additional values and/or principles do you exhibit consistently? Give examples:

   _____

   _____

   _____

   _____

3. Are there values listed that you discovered and believe you lack demonstrating consistently? Be specific and give examples when possible.

   _____

   _____

   _____

   _____

   _____

   _____

4. What are some of your personal values and/or principles that you would like to share or find ways to expand on through focus, and why are they important? Define if listed as a current value or new.

    _____

    _____

    _____

    _____

5. From your viewpoint, do you see that you consistently exhibit the values you listed that you would live by? Why or why not?

    _____

    _____

    _____

    _____

6. Why are values and principles important to you in regards to their internal customers, friends, peers, and associates?

    _____

    _____

    _____

    _____

7. Why are values and principles important to you in regards to their external customers, those who view you from a distance?

    _____

    _____

    _____

    _____

8. What are some of the best examples that other individuals display and exhibit their values and principles?

_____

_____

_____

_____

9. Who do you admire that demonstrates their values consistently and openly, and what quality of theirs would you like to adopt and develop?

_____

_____

_____

_____

10. Please rank the following values on a scale of 1 through 17

    A) Trust _____

    B) Integrity _____

    C) Honesty _____

    D) Ethics _____

    E) Respect _____

    F) Initiative _____

    G) Fun _____

    H) Celebration _____

    I) Achievement _____

    J) Accountability _____

    K) Knowledge _____

    L) Recognition _____

    M) Transparency _____

N) Excellence _____

O) Impact _____

P) Joy _____

Q) Courage _____

11. Please provide your perception on the contribution and impact that you make to the community according to your vision and goals driven by your values?

_____

_____

_____

_____

_____

12. Are you satisfied or would you like to improve? Explain:

_____

_____

_____

_____

_____

13. If your values remain as stated, are there areas you would like to focus on more to demonstrate these values more prominently? Explain:

_____

_____

_____

_____

_____

14. Is there a value(s) you would like to add to the current list, or alter a current one to expand on? Explain:

_____

_____

_____

_____

_____

15. Is there a current value you would like to eliminate from the list? Explain:

_____

_____

_____

_____

16. With any new value(s) listed please list a Principle Statement that you would like to adopt.

_____

_____

_____

_____

17. With any adjustments to your Values and Principles, are you committed to these as the foundation for you as an individual? Which, if any, may be a challenge? Explain:

_____

_____

_____

_____

Mission

18. Re-read your Mission Statement, does it still define your purpose and reason for existence? Explain why or why not?

_____

_____

_____

19. Does your mission still give purpose to your direction or does a new one need to be adopted to adjust to your development and growth and new stages personally and professionally? Explain why or why not?

_____

_____

_____

20. What are some of your new areas of focus that would drive your reason for existence and purpose for your achievements?

_____

_____

_____

21. Define if your mission needs altering, or a new mission creation that drives your direction based upon your growth, development, personal, and professional environment. List a few words that describe the changes.

_____

_____

_____

_____

_____

22. Write a new Mission Statement draft.

_____

_____

_____

_____

23. Review with mentors, peers, and trusted advisors. Write out a new Mission Statement to adopt.

_____

_____

_____

_____

Vision

24. Re-read your Vision Statement? Does it still guide your direction of achievement with a BHAG? Explain why or why not?

_____

_____

_____

_____

_____

25. If a new BHAG needs to be developed, what achievements would be considered? List up to 3.

_____

_____

_____

_____

_____

26. Write a new Vision Statement draft.

_____

_____

_____

_____

_____

27. Review with mentors, peers, and trusted advisors. Write out a new Vision Statement to adopt.

_____

_____

_____

_____

_____

* Review with your mentors and with those you mentor. Gain feedback, seek honesty, and value their comments and opinions. The exercise is not a mandate to change your values and principles, or Mission and Vision Statements, as they may still be effective for you. But it is an opportunity to embrace areas that need improvement, as well as additional areas to add if defined.

Ann's Values & Principles Survey Update:

Through the years, Ann excelled in demonstrating her values and principles. She exhibited her mission openly, so that everyone she came in contact with understood her reason for existence. On the evaluation document that I shared, the evaluation document and process covered Values and Principles, and also the evaluation of the Mission Statement and Vision Statement. The foundation of having mentors and mentoring others allowed her to demonstrate the importance of each value and principle, and also to develop strong resources for honest and direct feedback. Ann evaluated her Values and Principles, as well as her Mission and Vision Statements, around the 3-year mark as she was expanding personally and professionally with promotions, so the timing was fitting. The exercise feedback from her support network was well received. Ann realized she needed to expand on her value of fun, as a peer or two pointed out to Ann that sometimes she would place too much pressure on herself and that she would sacrifice on this value. The feedback was enlightening. The one value and principle statement she added was a Work-Life Balance. Through her mentors, she questioned where she could add this as a focus and not sacrifice success and accomplishments. One mentor advised and provided the feedback, that if Ann did not add a better work-life balance to her life that would alter their perception of her success, as accomplishments are much more valuable with a balanced life. This process helped Ann define a new Mission Statement, followed by a new Vision Statement which gave an outlook for the next 3 to 5 years. Ann created a new document that showcased her Values and Principles, defined a new monument word, *MOUNTAIN*, to memorize with the added Principle Statements, and she listed her new Mission Statement and Visions Statement.

In working with Ann as a mentor, I was pleased with how she stayed humble and focused and learned to be more decisive when decisions needed to be made and roadblocks were presented. Ann exhibited confidence and shared it with others. Within the first 3-years Ann was asked to teach others the process of building Values, Principles, Mission, and Vision Statements. She did this first with the North Chamber of Commerce, and in a short time it expanded over to Our Empowering Women. As she taught, she earned respect and her becoming a mentor to others developed with their trust in her knowledge and experiences. This played a vital role in her Mission Statement of, *To seek solutions and betterment of myself and others through compassion and effort, and to face the future with an optimistic outlook.* As she worked on her self-development, the development of others became more prevalent and it demonstrated to Ann as well as others of her leadership abilities. It is a known fact that individuals have an innate hunger to be led, and look for leaders to follow subconsciously. Ann had individuals gravitate to her natural leadership, within these support networks, as well as within her employment. With the process, her mentors as well as those she mentored, assisted Ann in defining a new Mission Statement that would adapt and adjust to her current state. *To Lead With A Passion For Success, That Develops Myself And Others To Maximize Their Gifts And Abilities To Overcome Challenges And Brings Positive Change.*

Within these 3 years, Ann worked through her challenges and stayed focused on her goals. Within her Vision Statement, she was able to earn one promotion within her employment and would be next in line for another when it presented itself. She had accomplished her savings percentage objective, and as she earned the next promotion she would have obtained her earning objective. Ann and her husband have since become the proud owners of their own home, which was well-deserved. Ann has found the opportunity to work with abused women as defined in her Vision Statement. This has been very rewarding as well as with those she mentors. Ann has updated her Vision Statement to, *To Lead And Develop My Own Business That Supports My Financial Goals And Is Focused On Personal Development Of Others. In Addition, To Elevate Income To Above $100,000 Per Year In Salary.*

Ann's Principle Statements

Maintain respect for others by earning and demonstrating respect daily.

Own the trust of your integrity through action always.

Understand a work-life balance is a measure of success.

No one is above accountability, starting with yourself.

Taste the hunger for what feeds you and drives you to the next level.

Always be driven by initiative and seek creativity and welcome new ideas.

Initiate joy, fun, and celebration of accomplishments large and small.

Natural passion drives daily achievement.

Ann's Mission Statement:

To Lead With A Passion For Success, That Develops Myself And Others To Maximize Their Gifts And Abilities To Overcome Challenges, And Brings Positive Change.

Ann's Vision Statement:

To Lead And Develop My Own Business That Supports My Financial Goals of $200,000 Plus In Annual Bottom-line Profit,

And Is Focused On Personal Development Of Others. *In Addition, To Elevate Income To Above $100,000 Per Year In Salary*

Ann's Continued Development & Success: Ride The Momentum

As Ann continued, she consistently executed her action plans, whether on development, initiatives, or goal achievement. Through mentorship and other education, she has learned and embraced that consistency comes from a strong foundation sustained by daily habits. As we executed in our evaluation of her personal and professional goals, Ann learned that a systematic evaluation and assessment process was important to keep objectives alive and breathing that drive ultimate achievement and success. She understood and then taught others, that success is about consistent execution to reach the mountaintop of achievement. However, to maintain that achievement, an individual must strive through the valleys that will appear through the journey. This is how one rides the momentum.

Over the next few years, Ann continued her growth and worked through obstacles. By mentoring others, she learned the value that while you mentor others you gain additional knowledge and perspective that allowed her to stay humble and grounded. When one has mentors, as well as those they mentor, this builds a continued hunger that one strives for achievement and development. Ann achieved her second promotion within our organization and flourished with her team and overall achievement. Soon Ann was being recruited by other organizations, yet eventually took the entrepreneurial route and started her own consulting business and grew it each year. She would speak at events, locally and in other cities. Ann consistently found other mentors to learn from and always paid it forward. She and her husband established a lifestyle they desired that provided well for their son, with a good education path. Ann excelled and surpassed her financial goals, and demonstrated the tenacity and perseverance to make any necessary adjustments to stay in alignment. Most rewarding was her commitment to the community, as Ann continued to work with abused women with her husband's participation. Ann's gratefulness has been demonstrated as she lives the model that great leaders pay it forward. After all, paying it forward helps drive the momentum. We all know, momentum is a powerful thing.

Download Free Workbook
with additional forms and worksheets
at www.markvillareal.com/aspiringwomen

www.ingramcontent.com/pod-product-compliance
Lightning Source LLC
Chambersburg PA
CBHW071157210326
41597CB00016B/1586